BEFORE THEY ASK

The Playbook for The Customer Sensor Economy
The Future of Customer Experience, Customer Technologies,
and Autonomous Self-Optimizing Systems

Michael R. Hoffman
Creator of the CxC Matrix Framework
Customer Worthy Publishing

Before They Ask, The Playbook for The Customer Sensor Economy

Customer Worthy Publishing | Basking Ridge, NJ

ISBN: 979-8-9952226-5-1 (paperback)

Printed in the United States of America

Table of Contents

APPENDICES

PREFACE

The Sensory Revolution: When the World Became the Interface

Your right hand contains approximately 100,000 nerve fibers. Each fingertip alone hosts more than 3,000 individual touch receptors — Meissner's corpuscles that detect the lightest brush of fabric, Merkel's disks that read surface texture, Pacinian corpuscles that sense vibration from two rooms away, Ruffini endings that map the angle and stretch of your grip. When you shake a stranger's hand, tens of thousands of these receptors fire simultaneously, generating millions of electrical signals in the few seconds of contact. Your brain synthesizes all of this into a single, coherent experience: warm, dry, firm, friendly.

Now consider your customer.

Your customer exists, at this moment, at the intersection of dozens of active sensor streams. Their wearable device records resting heart rate, skin temperature, and gait pattern. Their smartphone tracks location, purchase history, browsing behavior, and social network activity. Their home monitors energy consumption and appliance usage. Their vehicle logs driving patterns and predictive maintenance needs. Their employer's systems record productivity and workflow patterns. And layered above all of this, AI agents are actively negotiating, filtering, comparing, and deciding — often before any human is consciously aware a decision is being made.

This is the Customer Sensor economy. And it changes everything about how we think about customer experience.

> ***"In the Customer Sensor economy, every device, signal, and micro-interaction becomes either a monetizable asset or a competitive liability."***

When I wrote the first edition of Customer Worthy in 2010, I was sitting on hold with my cell phone provider, manually calculating the $99 billion in wasted customer time their 60 million subscribers experienced each year. The math was simple: 22 minutes average hold time, multiplied by the number of annual calls, valued at minimum wage. The number was staggering, but the methodology was manual. The problem was visible, but the solution was largely analog.

In 2025, as I dictated the first draft of this preface while my autonomous vehicle negotiated with the local electrical grid for optimal charging rates during my morning commute, I realized how completely the world had transformed. The problem I documented in 2010 — organizations failing to think like their customers — remains the central challenge of business. But the tools for solving it, the stakes of failing to solve it, and the opportunities available to those who master it have expanded by orders of magnitude.

The Scale of the Transformation

The statistics from 2024 and 2025 paint a picture of both crisis and opportunity. According to the National Customer Rage Survey, 74% of Americans experienced a product or service problem in the preceding year — the highest level ever recorded. Customer rage had more than tripled since 2020, with 43% of dissatisfied customers reporting they had raised their voice at a service agent. The survey estimated $887 billion in annual revenue at risk from poor complaint handling alone.

Yet simultaneously, McKinsey's research demonstrated that companies earning $1 billion annually can gain an additional $700 million within three years of meaningfully investing in customer experience improvements. Forrester's data showed that 86% of buyers will pay a premium for demonstrably superior experience. And Gartner's analysis predicted that by 2028, autonomous AI agents would handle more than 40% of all customer service interactions without human intervention.

The gap between the crisis and the opportunity has never been larger. And it is the companies who learn to think like their customers — not just occasionally, not just in quarterly strategy sessions, but continuously, autonomously, at machine speed and human scale — that will claim the opportunity.

What Is the Customer Sensor mesh?

The term "Customer Sensor Mesh" describes the emerging mesh of connected devices, AI agents, and data streams that surrounds every customer in the modern economy. It is not a single technology or platform. It is the aggregate of every signal that a customer generates — consciously and unconsciously — as they move through their daily life.

A customer sensor mesh is, in a sense, the digital nervous system of the modern consumer. Just as the 3,000 receptors in a single fingertip allow a human brain to read surface texture, temperature, pressure, and vibration simultaneously and synthesize them into a coherent experience, the customer sensor mesh allows companies to read behavioral, environmental, physiological, and transactional signals simultaneously and synthesize them into coherent, anticipatory service.

The analogy is deliberate. The human sensory system does not wait to be asked. It continuously monitors, continuously transmits, continuously integrates information and anticipates, calculates and simulates outcomes and actions . The brain does not poll the fingertips every few seconds to ask if anything is happening. The system is always on, always processing, always ready to respond. The Customer Sensor economy demands the same architecture from companies: always-on, always-learning systems that can detect customer need states before customers themselves can articulate them.

Sensory System	Biological Analog	Customer Sensor Equivalent
Light touch detection	Meissner's Corpuscles (3,000+ per fingertip)	Behavioral signal processing — micro-engagement tracking
Sustained pressure	Merkel's Disks	Purchase intent modeling — sustained attention analysis
Vibration and deep stimulus	Pacinian Corpuscles	Market signal detection — competitive and environmental monitoring
Position and stretch	Ruffini's Corpuscles	Journey state mapping — customer lifecycle positioning
Temperature	Thermoreceptors	Sentiment analysis — emotional temperature monitoring
Pain and risk	Nociceptors	Churn risk detection — friction and frustration identification
Proprioception	Muscle and joint sensors	Customer value orientation — lifetime value trajectory modeling

The CxC Matrix in the Age of Sensing

The Customer Experience CxC Matrix — the framework this book is built around — was originally designed to map customer interactions across 15 lifecycle stages and 6 interaction channels. That 15×6 grid of 90 cells, each containing 9 treatment objectives, gave organizations a language for thinking systematically about customer experience. It turned what had been an intuitive, inconsistent, departmentally fragmented activity into a disciplined operational framework.

In the Customer Sensor economy, the CxC Matrix 3.0 must expand to encompass new dimensions. The 90 cells remain, but each cell now contains four additional layers: Perception (how is the customer being sensed?), Cognition (how are those signals being interpreted?), Actuation (what response is being triggered?), and Emotion (how is the interaction being emotionally calibrated?). The 810 performance accountability points of the original matrix have expanded into a multi-dimensional accountability architecture capable of tracking performance across every possible combination of sensor input, AI response, and customer outcome.

This book is your guide to building that architecture. Whether you are a chief experience officer trying to understand your organization's strategic position, an innovation leader and transformation engineering leader designing the next generation of solutions to elevate experiences, grow revenue and differentiate at the point of customer, an operations leader trying to design more intelligent workflows, a technology leader trying to build the right infrastructure, or a practitioner trying to optimize individual customer interactions — the principles, frameworks, and case studies in this book will give you the foundation you need.

The Road Ahead: 2031 to 3038

Part IV of this book extends the Customer Sensor Mesh framework into the future — from the near-term wearable intelligence era to the speculations and predictions for the emerging Customer Sensor devices, integrations, services and experiences through 2040. These chapters are not science fiction. They are the logical extrapolation of trends already visible in 2026: the declining cost of sensors and their inclusion in every system, the increasing capability of AI, the expanding integration between physical and digital systems, and the accelerating autonomy of AI agents acting on behalf of human customers.

The 2040 scenario is, admittedly, speculative. But my solution and product design experience over the last 15 years has tremendously successful for organizations from financial services to wineries, from warehouses filled with a billion sheets of paper to the US Government exploring blockchain and mobile solutions for housing, finance, ESG, compliance and integrated, dynamic oversight, the discipline of thinking through the long arc of customer experience — of asking what the CxC Matrix would look like if every interaction were fully autonomous, fully personalized, and fully embedded in the physical environment — is itself valuable. It forces clarity about the principles that matter regardless of the technology: customer value creation, ethical data use, trust as competitive advantage, and the irreducible importance of human connection even in the most automated systems.

The hand with its 100,000 nerves does not exist to produce data. It exists to reach out, to grasp, to make contact with the world and to build, through accumulated touch, a relationship with reality. The Customer Sensor Mesh, at its best, serves the same purpose: not to extract data from customers, but to reach them more completely, to understand them more fully, and to serve them more genuinely than has ever before been possible.

That is what it means, in 2030 and beyond, to be Customer Worthy.

— Michael R. Hoffman

Basking Ridge, New Jersey

The Science of Sensing: What the Human Hand Teaches Us About Customer Experience

The human hand's sensory capabilities — those 100,000 nerves, those 3,000 receptors per fingertip — were not designed by evolution to collect data. They were designed to enable relationship: to allow one human being to understand another through touch, to build things together, to provide comfort and to receive it. The sophistication of the sensing architecture exists in service of the relationship, not as an end in itself.

When you shake someone's hand for the first time, you receive an extraordinary amount of information. The warmth or coolness of their palm tells you something about their circulatory state and their current physiological arousal. The firmness of their grip communicates confidence or its absence. The texture of their skin carries the history of their work. The duration of the handshake tells you something about their social comfort. The slight tremor that some people show tells you about their current emotional state. All of this, processed in milliseconds, contributes to the initial impression that will shape every subsequent interaction.

A handshake lasting just a few seconds could easily generate millions of distinct electrical signals that travel to the brain for processing. The brain does not experience these as millions of separate data points — it synthesizes them instantly into a single, rich, coherent impression. This synthesis — from millions of signals to one coherent experience — is the model for what excellent Customer Sensor Mesh systems should do.

The failure mode of early Customer Sensor implementations was to treat the sensing capability as the output rather than the input: to generate enormous volumes of customer data and then fail to synthesize it into something coherent, useful, and genuinely valuable for the customer and the organization. The organizations that struggle most with Customer Sensor transformation are those whose data infrastructure has grown faster than their analytical capability — who are sensing more than they can understand and understanding more than they can act on.

The organizations that succeed are those who maintain the discipline of the human sensory system: sensing precisely what is necessary, synthesizing instantly into coherent understanding, and converting that understanding into appropriate, proportionate, relationship-serving action. Not collecting data for its own sake. Not optimizing for metric performance as an end in itself. Using the extraordinary capabilities of the Customer Sensor Mesh infrastructure to reach customers more completely, understand them more fully, and serve them more genuinely than has ever before been possible.

That is the promise of this book. That is the purpose of the CxC Matrix 3.0. And that is what it means, in 2030 and beyond, to be truly Customer Worthy.

INTRODUCTION

The Quantum Customer: From Touchpoints to Sensor Clouds

At 7:14 AM on a Tuesday, Neil's autonomous SUV detected a slight vibration in the front axle bearing. Within 3.2 seconds, the vehicle's diagnostic AI analyzed vibration patterns against 17 million similar cases, predicted a 91% probability of bearing failure within 22 days, queried Neil's calendar for optimal service windows, negotiated with three certified repair centers for pricing and availability, secured a 15% loyalty discount by anonymously offering Neil's driving data to the winning shop, scheduled the appointment, added it to Neil's calendar, and notified his insurance company of the pending maintenance visit for warranty documentation purposes.

Neil only learned of this entire transaction when his dashboard displayed: "Front axle service scheduled for Thursday, 3 PM. Estimated savings: $212. Accept?"

This is not a hypothetical scenario from a distant future. This is the Customer Sensor Mesh economy already emerging now, and it will define competitive strategy for the next thirty years.

The Fundamental Premise Has Not Changed

Companies that continuously “think like a customer” outperform those that merely talk about it. This was true when I wrote the original Customer Worthy in 2010, when "thinking like a customer" meant training your call center representatives to listen rather than read scripts. It is true in 2025, when "thinking like a customer" means designing AI agents capable of anticipating needs that haven't yet been consciously formed. And it will be true in 2040, when — as this book's final chapter speculates — the distinction between customer and enterprise may be so thoroughly mediated by autonomous systems that the notion of a "transaction" will seem as quaint as a handwritten ledger entry.

The definition of "thinking like a customer" keeps expanding. That is the thesis of this book.

What Has Changed: Three Seismic Shifts

Shift 1: The Majority of Purchases Are Initiated by AI Agents

Recently, a number of technology advisory firms, gurus and technology forecasters predicted that more than 40% of all business-to-business purchasing decisions were being influenced or initiated by AI systems. By 2031, the majority of consumer purchases in categories ranging from commodity goods to utility services to financial products will be initiated not by human intention but by algorithmic prediction — your AI agent reordering household supplies before you know you need them, your vehicle negotiating service contracts before a part fails, your health management system scheduling preventive care before you experience symptoms.

The implication for the CxC Matrix is profound: the "customer" in many interaction cells is increasingly not a human being exercising conscious choice, but an AI agent executing a decision protocol. Designing customer experiences for these algorithmic customers — making your offerings readable, negotiable, and optimizable by machine systems — is now a primary competitive discipline.

Shift 2: The Average Consumer Actively and Passively Interacts with 30 to 48 Connected Devices Daily

In 2010, the average consumer owned two to three internet-connected devices. Now, that number has grown to more than 20 in developed markets, and the interaction count — not just ownership, but active data exchange — has reached 30 to 48 daily events for the typical connected consumer. By 2031, the proliferation of ambient computing, embedded sensors, and wearable technology will push this number well above 1000.

Each device interaction is a data signal. Each signal is an opportunity. And each opportunity missed is a competitive loss. The CxC Matrix 3.0 must account for this device ecosystem, mapping not just which channel a customer is using but which combination of physical, digital, hybrid, and synthetic contexts is shaping their experience at any given moment.

Shift 3: Customer Attention Can Be Measured, Valued, and Traded in Millisecond Increments

The femtosecond economy — the concept introduced in Chapter 6 of this book — describes the emerging market for human and AI attention at sub-second resolution. Today, programmatic advertising already trades in 100-millisecond increments. By 2031, attention valuation systems will operate at biometric resolution, pricing the cost of a customer's conscious focus against the projected lifetime value opportunity of each micro-interaction.

This is not dystopian. It is the logical extension of the principle that every interaction has economic value — a principle that lies at the heart of the original CxC Matrix. The difference is precision. Where the original framework helped organizations think clearly about which interactions mattered and why, the Customer Sensor Mesh framework enables them to act on that insight at machine speed, at the granularity of individual milliseconds, across the full ecosystem of customer touchpoints.

The CxC Matrix 3.0 as Operating System

The CxC Matrix 3.0 that forms the backbone of this book is not merely an updated version of a consulting framework. It is an operating system — a structured architecture for making decisions about customer experience that can be executed by humans, automated by AI, and continuously optimized through machine learning.

The original 15 lifecycle stages remain: Awareness, Information, Identification, Selection, Negotiation, Contract, Logistics, Delivery, Acceptance, Collection, Use, Care/Support, Repair, Disposal, and Community. The 6 interaction channels — Geographic, Digital, Location-Based, Third-Party, One-on-One, and Community — remain as well. What the 3.0 framework adds are the four cognitive processing layers (Perception, Cognition, Actuation, Emotion) that transform each of the 90 cells from a static descriptor into a dynamic decision engine.

The CxC Matrix 3.0 at a Glance

15 Customer Lifecycle Stages × 6 Interaction Channels = 90 Interaction Cells. Each cell contains: 9 Treatment Objectives × 4 Cognitive Processing Layers × N Sensor Input Streams = 810+ Performance Accountability Points per session, per customer, per channel. The VMAO Cycle (Visualize, Monetize, Analyze, Optimize) drives continuous improvement across every cell. The result: a unified operational language for every department, every system, and every AI agent engaged in customer experience management.

How to Read This Book

Customer Worthy: Customer Sensor Mesh is organized into four parts that progress from foundational concepts through practical frameworks to transformational strategy and future vision.

Part I: The Customer Sensor Mesh Revolution (Chapters 1–3) establishes the core concepts: what the Customer Sensor Mesh is and how it operates, how the CxC Matrix 3..0 expands to encompass its new dimensions, and what "thinking like a customer" means when customers exist simultaneously across physical, digital, and synthetic domains.

Part II: Capturing and Optimizing Experience (Chapters 4–7) gets practical, exploring how to manage the Four Domains of Customer Reality, capture immersive experience streams, operate in the femtosecond attention economy, and build event-driven experience pipelines that function as living operational code.

Part III: The Nine Requirements (Chapters 8–10) revisits the core CxC Matrix treatment objectives — Identify, Recognize, Fulfill, Upgrade, Cross-Sell, Expand, Educate, Collect, and Generate Referrals — through the lens of digital twin technology, living customer schematics, and multi-agent trust ecosystems.

Part IV: Quantum Customer Transformation (Chapters 11–16) projects the Customer Sensor Mesh framework forward: from the wearable intelligence era of 2030–2035 through the digitally aware built environment of 2035–2040, the emergence of self-programming customer systems, and the organizational transformation required to lead in this new landscape.

You do not need to read this book in sequence. Customer experience engineers building their 2030 strategy may want to begin with Chapters 1, 4, and 14. Technology leaders assessing infrastructure requirements will find Chapters 6, 7, and 13 most immediately useful. Executives thinking about the longer arc of competitive strategy will want to start with Part IV and work backward.

Wherever you start, remember Neil and his SUV bearing. The future of customer experience is not about technology. It is about the 17 systems that worked before Neil woke up so that his day could begin without friction, without worry, and with $212 of value delivered before he had finished his first cup of coffee. That is what it means to think like a customer. That is what it means to be Customer Worthy.

Neil's Morning, Fully Mapped: A CxC Matrix Analysis

Neil's Tuesday morning — the 17 systems that worked before he woke — is worth examining in full CxC Matrix detail, because it illustrates how the Customer Sensor Mesh framework applies to a real-world scenario at every level of the matrix architecture.

System 1 (6:10 PM Monday): Neil's vehicle's predictive maintenance AI detects the bearing vibration pattern while he is driving home from work. This is a Perception Layer event at Stage 12 (Care/Support) × Channel 3 (Location — the vehicle as a mobile physical environment). The system correctly identifies the customer state (Neil is the owner of a 2029 Volvo EX90 with 34,000 miles, a premium service contract, and a strong preference for minimal friction in maintenance management) and initiates the resolution process.

System 2 (6:10–6:11 PM Monday): The vehicle's Cognition Layer analyzes the bearing signal against 17 million comparable cases in the fleet database. It determines 91% probability of bearing failure within 22 days — urgency level: moderate. This triggers the actuation protocol for Stage 12 × Location.

System 3 (6:11 PM Monday): The vehicle AI queries Neil's digital calendar through the household AI integration layer. It identifies three potential service windows in the next two weeks that meet Neil's standing preferences: morning appointments that end by 10 AM, avoiding Friday appointments, and preferring certified dealers within 15 minutes of his home address.

System 4-6 (6:11-6:13 PM Monday): The vehicle AI queries three certified repair centers within 15 minutes of Neil's home, checking real-time appointment availability for each of his three preferred windows. Two centers have availability; one does not.

System 7 (6:13 PM Monday): The vehicle AI initiates a negotiation protocol with both available service centers through their MCP-compliant booking APIs, for need/function-specific ecosystem mapping. It presents Neil's vehicle identifier, the diagnostic report, the service history (which includes the 15% loyalty discount earned through the authorized maintenance program), and the three preferred time windows. Both centers submit automated quotes.

System 8 (6:14 PM Monday): The household AI negotiation engine evaluates the two quotes. Center A offers a lower base price; Center B offers a slightly higher price but includes a diagnostic upload that will extend the vehicle's predictive maintenance model accuracy. Neil's AI, having been configured to value service quality over minimal cost for vehicle maintenance, selects Center B and confirms the Thursday 8 AM appointment.

System 9 (6:14 PM Monday): The confirmed appointment is written to Neil's calendar, a reminder is set for Wednesday evening, and a parking reservation at Center B's customer lot is made through the mobility management system.

System 10 (6:15 PM Monday): Neil's insurance carrier receives an automated notification of the scheduled maintenance event, which updates the vehicle's warranty documentation record and confirms that the scheduled work meets warranty maintenance requirements.

System 11 (11:47 PM Monday): Neil's household finance AI reviews the day's scheduled transactions, including the vehicle service appointment. It notes that the service cost ($847) will be partially covered by the premium maintenance contract ($500 coverage) and flags the net $347 out-of-pocket cost as within Neil's established home maintenance budget allocation. No action required.

System 12 (6:07 AM Tuesday): Neil's morning routine AI initiates the household wakeup sequence. Based on Neil's Tuesday morning patterns (typically leaves for work between 7:15 and 7:45 AM), it begins the gradual bedroom lighting increase at 6:47 AM.

System 13 (6:47 AM Tuesday): Neil's smartwatch detects the transition from deep sleep to light sleep — the optimal wakeup window. The bedroom lighting system receives the signal and begins the gradual brightening sequence.

System 14 (6:52 AM Tuesday): Neil's kitchen AI detects motion in the bedroom (Neil has risen) and begins the coffee brewing sequence using Neil's weekday morning preference profile (medium strength, large cup, no foam).

System 15 (6:58 AM Tuesday): Neil's phone receives a morning briefing notification that includes the vehicle service appointment on Thursday and a brief summary of what the repair will involve — enough that Neil can describe it accurately if his partner asks what the appointment is for.

System 16 (7:01 AM Tuesday): The vehicle service center's customer communication AI sends Neil a pre-appointment welcome message that confirms the appointment details, provides directions to the service center, describes the loaner vehicle options available if the repair requires more than one day, and offers a link to a live status tracker that will update him throughout the repair process.

System 17 (7:14 AM Tuesday): Neil's dashboard displays: "Front axle service scheduled for Thursday, 3 PM. Estimated savings: $212. Accept?" Neil taps Accept while sipping his coffee.

> ***"Seventeen systems. Zero friction. $212 saved. One confirmation tap. That is what it means to think like a customer in 2031."***

The CxC Matrix 3.0 analysis of Neil's morning reveals the breadth of lifecycle stages and channels involved in a single, apparently simple service event. Stages 12 (Care/Support), 13 (Repair), 7 (Logistics), 6 (Contract), and 10 (Payment/Collection) are all touched within a 13-hour period. Channels 3 (Location), 2 (Digital), 4 (Third-Party), and 5 (One-on-One) are all engaged — the vehicle environment, the digital calendar and booking infrastructure, the third-party service centers and insurance carrier, and the household AI's personalized management of Neil's preferences and budget.

The nine treatment objectives at work include Identify (Neil's vehicle is correctly identified across all systems), Recognize (his preferences, maintenance history, and loyalty status are applied throughout), Fulfill (the bearing is being serviced before it fails), Educate (Neil receives just enough information to feel informed without being overwhelmed), Collect (the diagnostic data improves the fleet's predictive maintenance models), and Generate Referrals (the seamless experience creates the emotional conditions for Neil to recommend this vehicle brand and service network to others).

What makes this example instructive is not its sophistication — by 2031 standards, it will be routine. What makes it instructive is its completeness: every element of the interaction was designed for Neil's outcome rather than the company's convenience. The appointment time works for Neil's schedule. The service center was selected based on Neil's quality preferences, not the system's cost minimization. The communication volume was calibrated to Neil's preference for minimal friction rather than the service center's preference for comprehensive pre-appointment communication. The entire architecture was built around the question: "What does Neil need, and how can we deliver it with the least possible friction at the highest possible quality?" That question — asked and answered 17 times before Neil took his first sip of coffee — is the Customer Sensor operating philosophy made real.

PART I: THE CUSTOMER SENSOR REVOLUTION

When Everything Senses, Everything Sells

CHAPTER ONE

Customer Sensor Mesh Commerce

When Your Car, Home, and Office Form a Customer Experience Network

The Invisible Conversation

Neil's Tuesday morning began not with an alarm but with a cascade of autonomous negotiations conducted on his behalf while he slept. His autonomous vehicle had detected axle bearing wear patterns. His home energy system had negotiated overnight charging rates with the grid. His health monitor had synchronized his sleep data with his digital twin's predictive wellness model and flagged a slightly elevated cortisol pattern for review. His grocery management system had identified three items below threshold inventory and placed purchase orders with two competing delivery services, selecting the winner based on price, proximity, and carbon footprint scoring.

By the time Neil's bedroom lights gradually brightened at 6:47 AM — his preferred wake pattern, learned from three months of sleep data — 17 separate automated systems had already executed decisions on his behalf. None of them required his input. All of them created measurable value.

This is the invisible conversation of the Customer Sensor economy. It is a continuous, multi-party negotiation conducted at machine speed, on behalf of human principals, across a mesh of connected devices, AI agents, and data streams. For businesses, it represents the most significant shift in customer relationship management since the invention of the telephone.

From IoT to Customer Sensor Mesh

The Internet of Things was the first chapter of this story. Beginning in the early 2000s and accelerating dramatically through the 2010s and 2020s, IoT connected billions of physical objects to internet infrastructure — thermostats, appliances, vehicles, medical devices, industrial equipment. The data these objects generated was, initially, largely descriptive: temperature readings, usage logs, location pings. Useful, but passive.

The Customer Sensor Mesh is what IoT becomes when it is coupled with artificial intelligence, machine learning, autonomous agents, and the Model Context Protocol (MCP) — the emerging standard for machine-to-machine communication that allows AI systems to discover, negotiate with, and transact through other AI systems. The shift is from passive data collection to active value creation. From "your thermostat recorded that the temperature was 72 degrees" to "your home management system negotiated a 12% discount on your utility contract based on your usage patterns and competing provider offers."

The components of the Customer Sensor Mesh operate on four layers:

Mesh Layer	Function	Technology Drivers	Business Impact
Signal Layer	Capture intent, behavioral, and environmental signals	IoT sensors, wearables, cameras, RFID, edge AI	Continuous situational awareness at machine speed

Mesh Layer	Function	Technology Drivers	Business Impact
Intent Layer	Filter, prioritize, and interpret signals for action	LLMs, behavioral models, preference graphs	Anticipatory service before conscious customer request
Negotiation Layer	Autonomous value exchange between AI agents	MCP, smart contracts, dynamic pricing engines	Optimized transaction outcomes without human friction
Execution Layer	Self-optimizing fulfillment and delivery	Robotics, autonomous logistics, API orchestration	Frictionless service delivery at scale

The Permission Architecture

The Customer Sensor Mesh operates within a permission architecture — a layered consent framework that governs what autonomous actions each device and agent may take on a customer's behalf. Today, this architecture is still largely implicit, encoded in terms-of-service agreements and device configuration settings that few consumers carefully review. By 2031, permission architecture will be a central competitive differentiator: customers will actively choose between companies that give them granular, legible control over their autonomous agents and those that obscure or exploit the permission relationship.

The permission architecture has four tiers. At Tier 1, the device or agent may monitor and report but cannot take action without explicit human approval. At Tier 2, the device may take routine, low-stakes actions (reordering common household items, scheduling maintenance below a dollar threshold) without approval. At Tier 3, the device may negotiate and transact within defined parameters (price ranges, preferred vendors, service quality thresholds). At Tier 4 — the level at which Neil's 17 morning systems operate — the device has significant autonomous authority, with human override available but rarely exercised.

The CxC Matrix 3.0 in the Customer Sensor Economy

The CxC Matrix must now account for interactions that occur before any human is aware of them. Consider the traditional matrix cell: Awareness Stage × Digital Channel. In the pre-Sensor economy, this cell represented a human customer discovering a brand through a search engine or social media post — a conscious act of attention and engagement.

In the Customer Sensor economy, the Awareness Stage × Digital Channel cell also contains machine-level awareness events: an AI purchasing agent discovering a vendor through an API marketplace, a predictive system identifying a product category need based on consumption patterns, a competitive intelligence algorithm flagging a pricing opportunity. These machine awareness events may eventually lead to a human becoming aware, or they may complete an entire purchase cycle without direct human involvement.

> **CX Leader Prompt: Mapping Machine Awareness**
>
> Audit your current customer awareness programs. For each channel and awareness trigger, ask: "Could this awareness event be generated by an AI agent acting on a customer's behalf, rather than by the customer directly?" For each cell where the answer is yes, design a machine-readable awareness pathway — structured data, API endpoints, and negotiation protocols that make your offering discoverable and evaluable by autonomous purchasing systems.

Hypothetical Case Study: Health Service Provider Patient Sensor Mesh

In 2029, a regional health system deployed what they called a Patient Sensor Health Mesh — an integrated network connecting wearable devices, home environmental sensors, electronic health records, and AI diagnostic systems for enrolled patients with chronic conditions. The system was designed not to replace clinical judgment but to extend clinical awareness into the spaces between scheduled appointments.

The results demonstrated the potential of the Customer Sensor model applied to healthcare. When a patient's wearable detected an anomalous cardiac rhythm pattern, the system correlated the signal with medication timing data, recent activity levels, and environmental factors. It consulted a digital twin simulation model to assess the probability distribution of clinical outcomes. Based on that analysis, it either scheduled a telemedicine consultation within four hours, escalated to emergency services, or adjusted the patient's care protocol within established clinical parameters — all without requiring the patient to notice their own symptoms.

The health system reported a 27% reduction in preventable emergency department visits among enrolled patients, a 34% improvement in chronic disease management outcomes, and a 15% reduction in overall care costs for the enrolled population. Patient satisfaction scores increased by 22 points. The system worked not because it replaced clinical expertise but because it extended clinical sensing into the continuous fabric of patients' daily lives.

The CxC Matrix 3.0 structure that governed this system is directly applicable to any industry deploying Customer Sensor Mesh capabilities:

1. Define the signal set: What signals, from what sources, are relevant to each lifecycle stage of the customer relationship?
2. Map the interpretation logic: For each signal pattern, what does it mean about the customer's current state, needs, and likely future trajectory?
3. Design the action protocols: For each interpretive conclusion, what response is appropriate? At what level of confidence? With what degree of autonomy?
4. Establish permission boundaries: What actions require explicit approval? What can proceed autonomously within standing consent?
5. Build the feedback loop: How does outcome data refine the interpretation and action protocols over time?

AI as Your Digital Customer Advocate

In the Customer Sensor economy, AI occupies a dual role that has no historical precedent. It simultaneously serves as the customer's agent — anticipating needs, filtering options, negotiating terms — and as the company's operational engine — identifying opportunities, optimizing interactions, managing fulfillment. This dual-role architecture creates a new competitive dynamic: the best customer experiences will be those where the customer's AI agent and the company's AI system reach mutually beneficial outcomes efficiently.

Companies that understand this dynamic will invest not just in their own AI capabilities but in making their systems legible and trustworthy to customers' AI agents. Machine-readable product data, transparent pricing APIs, auditable decision logic, and reliable performance metrics will become the primary raw materials of customer acquisition in automated purchasing environments.

Early Market Indicators for Customer Sensor Competitive Advantage

Five metrics will define Customer Sensor competitiveness in the early adoption period of Today–2031:

- API Call Volume and MCP Solutions: A sustained increase in programmatic interactions with your products indicates growing integration with customer AI agents. Companies seeing 30%+ year-over-year growth in automated inquiry volume are winning the machine-awareness competition.
- Algorithm Preference Rate: When AI purchasing agents evaluate competing vendors, what percentage of automated selection events result in

your offering being chosen? This is the machine-world equivalent of market share, and it will diverge increasingly from human-driven market share as automation expands.

- Predictive Accuracy Index: How accurately do your systems anticipate customer needs before explicit requests? Each correctly anticipated need represents zero friction cost and maximum conversion probability. Companies achieving 70%+ predictive accuracy in high-frequency categories gain compounding advantage.
- Permission Depth Score: What level of autonomous decision-making authority do customers grant to your service? Higher permission levels indicate deeper trust and create defensible competitive position — customers with Tier 3 and Tier 4 permission relationships are dramatically less likely to churn.
- Sensor Integration Breadth: How many third-party data streams does your customer experience platform integrate? Each additional integration source improves prediction accuracy, deepens permission relationships, and increases switching cost.

Building Your Customer Sensor Mesh: A Step-by-Step Implementation Guide

The transition from traditional CX management to Customer Sensor operations is not a technology deployment — it is a transformation of operational philosophy. Organizations that approach it as a technology project consistently underperform expectations; organizations that approach it as a philosophical transformation consistently exceed them. The following step-by-step guide provides the operational sequence for building Customer Sensor capability in an organization that is starting from a solid but pre-Sensor CX foundation.

Step 1: Map Your Current Signal Landscape (Weeks 1-4)

Before deploying any new sensing capabilities, it is essential to understand what signals you are already collecting, how they are currently being used, and where the most significant gaps exist. Many organizations are surprised to discover that they are already collecting far more potentially useful sensor data than they are currently analyzing — data that sits in disparate systems, is collected by one department and unavailable to others, or is captured but never processed for customer experience insights.

The signal landscape audit examines six categories of currently available data: behavioral data from digital channels, transactional data from CRM and billing systems, service interaction data from support platforms, product usage data from connected products or SaaS platforms, third-party data from partnerships and data marketplaces, and operational data from internal systems that may have indirect customer experience implications. For each category, the audit documents what data is available, at what level of granularity, with what latency, and with what current analytical application. If you have mapped systems using the original Customer Experience Matrix design, use those maps and create a drop down to record the signal data.

Step 2: Identify the Ten Highest-Value Sensing Opportunities (Weeks 3-6)

Armed with the signal landscape audit, the next step is to identify the ten specific sensing opportunities that offer the highest combination of customer value and business impact. A sensing opportunity is a specific customer context — defined by lifecycle stage, channel, and customer segment — where adding or better analyzing sensor data would enable meaningfully better customer outcomes and measurably better business results.

The prioritization framework for sensing opportunities combines four factors: Frequency (how many customers encounter this context, and how often?), Impact (what is the potential improvement in customer outcome if sensing is added?), Feasibility (how readily available is the relevant sensor data, and how complex is the analytical challenge?), and Trust Risk (what is the risk that adding sensing here would feel intrusive or would require sensitive data that customers may not want to share?). The ten opportunities that score highest on the combined framework become the initial sensing roadmap.

Step 3: Design the Permission Architecture (Weeks 4-8)

Before deploying any new sensing capability, the permission architecture for that capability must be designed. This means identifying the customer benefit that the sensing capability enables, designing the consent flow that makes that benefit and the associated data collection transparent and controllable, and building the technical infrastructure that enforces the permission grants in practice.

The permission architecture design must be completed before technical deployment — not as a subsequent compliance step. Organizations that design permission architecture after building sensing systems typically find that the system design creates implicit data collection and processing patterns that cannot be adequately governed by a consent overlay, requiring expensive redesign to achieve genuine privacy-by-design architecture.

Step 4: Deploy, Measure, and Iterate (Weeks 6-26)

With permission architecture in place, the first sensing capabilities can be deployed in controlled pilot environments. The pilot deployment should be designed as a rigorous measurement experiment: clear hypotheses about the customer outcomes and business results expected from the sensing capability, well-defined metrics for measuring those outcomes, appropriate comparison groups for baseline measurement, and predetermined evaluation criteria that will guide the decision about whether to scale, modify, or discontinue the capability.

The iteration cycle for Customer Sensor capabilities is typically much shorter than for traditional CX initiatives — because the sensing infrastructure itself provides the feedback data needed to evaluate and improve performance. A well-designed Customer Sensor Mesh pilot can generate actionable performance data within days, compared to months for traditional campaign-based CX initiatives. This rapid feedback loop enables organizations to learn quickly, adjust confidently, and scale what works with evidence rather than intuition.

Implementation Trap: The Data Richness Illusion

Organizations deploying Customer Sensor Mesh capabilities for the first time frequently fall into the Data Richness Illusion: the assumption that more data automatically leads to better outcomes. In practice, more data creates analytical complexity that can actually degrade performance if the analytical infrastructure is not prepared to handle it. The organizations that achieve the best outcomes from their initial Customer Sensor Mesh deployments are those that focus intensely on a small number of high-value sensing signals and build deep analytical capability around each one before expanding the signal set. Start with the most important signal for the highest-value context. Get that right. Then expand.

Hypothetical Case Study: nAmazon's Household AI Consortium

By 2028, nAmazon had assembled what internal teams called the Household AI Consortium — an integrated ecosystem of nAlexa, nRing, nAmazon Fresh, nPrime Video, nAmazon Health, and nAmazon Financial Services that shared customer behavioral signals across product lines to create a unified household experience model. The consortium architecture allowed each service to understand not just a customer's behavior within its own domain but the full household context in which that behavior occurred.

When nAmazon Fresh detected that a household's food purchasing patterns had shifted toward specialty dietary products over a 30-day period, this signal was shared with nAmazon Health, which proactively surfaced relevant health information and related products. When nRing detected an unusual pattern of nighttime activity in a household whose primary resident was elderly, this signal was shared with nAmazon Health's caregiving services, which reached out proactively to confirm the resident's wellbeing. When nPrime Video consumption patterns in a household shifted significantly — less evening viewing, different content categories — this signal informed nAmazon Financial Services' assessment of whether to proactively adjust credit offerings.

The Household AI Consortium achieved dramatic results: household lifetime value 47% higher than non-consortium customers, service cross-utilization 3.2 times higher, and churn rates 62% lower. The consortium also generated significant controversy regarding the appropriateness of cross-service data sharing, leading nAmazon to implement an explicit Household Data Governance Framework that gave customers granular control over which services could share data with each other and for what purposes. The Household AI Consortium is instructive both as a model of the commercial potential of Customer Sensor integration and as a cautionary tale about the trust risks of data integration at scale.

Customer Sensor Applications Across Industries

The Customer Sensor Mesh framework is industry-agnostic in its principles but industry-specific in its implementation. Each sector presents unique combinations of customer relationship characteristics, regulatory constraints, sensing opportunities, and value creation mechanisms that shape how the framework is applied. The following sector profiles examine how leading organizations are building Customer Sensor capabilities in five major industry contexts, each illustrating distinct aspects of the framework in action.

Financial Services: The Intelligence Advantage

Financial services is the sector where Customer Sensor Mesh capabilities have the most direct and measurable impact on core business outcomes. Lending, insurance, investment management, and retail banking all involve high-stakes decisions by customers with incomplete information, high anxiety, and strong preference for advisors they can trust. The Customer Sensor Mesh organization that can anticipate customers' financial needs, deliver relevant information at the right moment, and provide genuinely personalized guidance creates a competitive advantage that traditional financial services organizations — constrained by branch networks, legacy technology, and product-centric sales cultures — find difficult to replicate.

The distinctive challenge in financial services Customer Sensor Mesh implementation is the regulatory environment. Financial services regulations in every major market impose specific requirements on how customer data can be used in product recommendation, pricing, and underwriting decisions. Fair lending laws prohibit using certain demographic attributes — race, religion, national origin, gender — in credit decisions. Suitability regulations require that investment product recommendations be demonstrably appropriate for a specific customer's situation and risk tolerance. Privacy regulations impose specific consent and retention requirements for financial data. The Customer Sensor Mesh organization in financial services must build its architecture with regulatory compliance as a first-class design requirement, not a post-hoc overlay.

The most successful Customer Sensor Mesh implementations in financial services share three characteristics. They are built around the customer's financial lifecycle — the predictable sequence of financial events and decisions that characterizes a customer's relationship with money over their lifetime — rather than around the organization's product catalog. They use anticipatory sensing to identify customers approaching major financial lifecycle transitions — homeownership readiness, education planning, retirement planning onset, generational responsibilities and care, inheritance receipt, income disruption — before those transitions become crises. And they invest in the human-AI collaboration infrastructure that allows financial advisors to perform at their best, augmented by AI customer intelligence rather than replaced by automated recommendation engines.

Retail and E-Commerce: The Frictionless Commerce Model

Retail and e-commerce represents the highest-velocity Customer Sensor Mesh environment — the sector where micro-moment optimization has the most immediate and measurable commercial impact, and where the gap between organizations with mature Customer Sensor Mesh capabilities and those without is most visibly expressed in business performance.

The fundamental value proposition of Customer Sensor Mesh in retail is the elimination of the friction gap — the difference between what customers want and what they can efficiently find, evaluate, and purchase. In the traditional retail environment, the friction gap was filled by knowledgeable store staff who could understand a customer's needs and guide them to the right product. As retail shifted to self-service digital channels, human guidance was lost, replaced by search algorithms that could match keywords but could not understand context, intent, or the unstated dimensions of customer need.

The Customer Sensor Mesh retail model is rebuilding the intelligence of human guidance at digital scale. The system that understands not just what a customer searched for but why they searched for it — the underlying problem they are trying to solve, the context in which they will use the product, the constraints that must be respected — can provide guidance that exceeds what even a skilled human salesperson could achieve without the benefit of real-time behavioral data and predictive modeling.

The leading retail Customer Sensor Mesh implementations have moved beyond personalized product recommendation to what might be called contextual commerce: the ability to understand the customer's complete situation, discussed as part of Total Consumption Economic Theory in Customer Worthy, now factored by customer and family lifestage at any given moment and assemble a solution — product, configuration, complementary items, services, financing, and fulfillment — that addresses the full context rather than just the stated request. A customer who searches for "wedding gift under $200" on a Friday afternoon is likely in a specific situation (the wedding is this weekend) that the Customer Sensor Mesh system can infer and respond to: inventory confirmation for same-day dispatch, gift wrapping options, personalized card composition assistance, and a delivery tracking link they can forward to the recipient. This is contextual commerce — assembling a complete solution rather than returning a product list.

Healthcare: The Continuous Care Model

Healthcare is the sector where Customer Sensor Mesh capabilities carry the highest stakes and the most profound value creation potential. The traditional healthcare model is episodic: patients interact with the healthcare system at discrete points — annual check-ups, acute illness visits, specialist referrals — with minimal monitoring or engagement in the spaces between. This episodic model is demonstrably suboptimal for managing the chronic conditions that drive the majority of healthcare costs and patient suffering: diabetes, cardiovascular disease, mental health conditions, and the complex, multi-system health challenges that characterize aging populations.

The Customer Sensor Mesh healthcare model deepens services situational understanding to include the patient's family members, their roles, capabilities, situations, caregivers roles and capabilities, and community ecosystem,: healthcare services, specialties, services. The Trust protocols discussed prior are designed into the patient's and caregivers Trust and Permission networks as required by law and as specified by each entity on the patient's defined care circle.

The Customer Sensor Mesh healthcare model replaces episodic care with continuous care: the integration of wearable monitoring, AI-powered health analytics, communications, and proactive care management to maintain a real-time awareness of each patient's health trajectory and intervene before problems become crises. The value creation potential is substantial: research across multiple health systems has demonstrated that predictive intervention programs based on continuous monitoring can reduce preventable hospitalization by 25–35%, improve chronic disease management outcomes by 20–40%, and reduce overall per-patient care costs by 15–25%. (Hypothetical estimates)

The healthcare sector also presents the most stringent privacy and ethical requirements for Customer Sensor Mesh implementation. Health data is the most sensitive category of personal information, and the consequences of breach, misuse, or discriminatory application can be severe — both for individual patients, their care circle and for the organizations responsible for the data. Healthcare Customer Sensor Mesh programs must be designed from the ground up with privacy-by-design principles, explicit informed consent for every data collection modality, and robust security architecture that anticipates adversarial attempts to exploit health data for insurance discrimination, employment discrimination, or other harmful purposes.

Automotive and Mobility: The Vehicle as Customer Platform

The connected vehicle is among the most commercially significant Customer Sensor Mesh platforms today. Modern vehicles generate enormous volumes of operational data — engine telemetry, location history, driving behavior patterns, infotainment usage, occupancy sensing — that, combined with owner demographic and behavioral data, creates a customer intelligence platform of exceptional richness. The commercial applications range from the immediate (Neil's bearing replacement scenario) to the long-term (using driving behavior data to underwrite insurance, predict purchase timing, and design next-generation vehicle features).

The mobility sector's Customer Sensor Mesh architecture is unique in that the primary sensing device — the vehicle itself — is a capital asset that customers own and maintain a long-term relationship with. The vehicle manufacturer has a direct relationship with the customer that extends over the full vehicle ownership period, typically 5–10 years, and through multiple ownership cycles if the customer remains loyal to the brand. The Customer Sensor Mesh capabilities built into the vehicle platform, create the foundation for a continuous relationship that compounds in value over the full ownership period — and potentially across multiple vehicle purchases if the permission relationship and trust equity are maintained.

The most advanced automotive Customer Sensor Mesh implementations are using vehicle data not just for operational optimization (predictive maintenance, over-the-air feature updates) but for lifestyle intelligence — understanding how customers use their vehicles in the context of their broader lives, and using that understanding to deepen relationships across the full ecosystem of customer needs that vehicle ownership intersects. I expect that automotive Customer Sensor Mesh will begin to capture and use multiple passenger profiles and environment observational data to continue to enhance customer experiences. Imagine a family member oassenger in need of medical assistance, connected via mesh sensor design to medical history and devices alerting hospital, care team, care circle, reserved hospital room space prepared for arrival in 20 minutes. Or, a customer who consistently uses their vehicle for early-morning exercise commutes is revealing information about their health and wellness orientation that a health insurance partner, a sports nutrition brand, or a premium athletic gear retailer might find highly relevant. The permission architecture governing this data sharing must be explicit and genuinely customer-controlled — but the commercial value of consensual lifestyle data integration is substantial.

Technology and SaaS: The Engagement Depth Model

Software-as-a-Service is the sector where Customer Sensor Mesh principles are most directly integrated with the product itself. In SaaS, the product is a digital service delivered through a digital interface — meaning that every customer interaction with the product is, by definition, a digital sensor mesh event. The usage analytics infrastructure that tracks feature adoption, session length, workflow patterns, and user engagement is the foundational Customer Sensor Mesh layer for every SaaS business, whether or not it is explicitly conceptualized in those terms.

The distinctive value creation opportunity in SaaS Customer Sensor Mesh implementation is engagement depth optimization: the use of behavioral analytics and AI-driven intervention to ensure that every customer achieves the maximum possible value from the product capabilities they have purchased. The business case is compelling: SaaS research consistently demonstrates that feature adoption depth is the strongest predictor of renewal, expansion, and advocacy behavior. Customers who have adopted more features, who use the product more frequently, and who have integrated it more deeply into their workflows are dramatically less likely to churn than customers who use only the entry-level features of a product they are technically subscribed to.

The Customer Sensor Mesh SaaS depiction in the 3.0 CxC Matrix, gains tremendously valuable information from the Digital and Community intersections where customers, companies, and ecosystems interact and agent based deployments and future "digitally-organic" designs are likely to emerge as organically designed SaaS functions and capabilities,

The Customer Sensor SaaS organization uses behavioral data to identify customers at every point in the engagement depth spectrum and design interventions appropriate to each. New customers in the first 30 days receive guided onboarding interventions timed to their actual behavioral patterns rather than to a fixed calendar. Customers who have been using the product for six months but show shallow feature adoption receive discovery interventions that introduce advanced capabilities contextually — at the moment when their current workflow would benefit most from the feature being introduced. Customers whose usage patterns show early churn signals receive proactive success outreach that diagnoses the underlying challenge and offers targeted support.

CHAPTER TWO

The CxC Matrix 3.0

Visualize · Analyze · Monetize · Prioritize · Optimize

Beyond the Grid: The Four-Dimensional Matrix

The original CxC Customer Experience Matrix mapped customer interactions across two dimensions: 15 customer lifecycle stages on the vertical axis, and 6 interaction channels on the horizontal axis. This produced 90 cells — each representing a distinct combination of "where the customer is in their relationship with the company" and "how they are currently engaging." Each cell contained 9 treatment objectives, producing 810 discrete performance accountability points.

This was a powerful framework for 2025, when most customer interactions were either human-to-human or human-to-digital. In the Customer Sensor economy of 2031, it is necessary but insufficient. The Matrix 3.0 adds two new dimensions — cognitive processing layers and sensor input streams — that transform each of the 90 cells from a static planning grid into a dynamic decision architecture.

The Four Cognitive Processing Layers

Every cell in the Matrix 3.0 now contains four processing layers that must be explicitly designed and managed:

Layer	Function	Core Technology	Key Design Question
Perception	Capture signals from all channels and devices	Edge AI, computer vision, IoT sensors, biometrics	What signals tell us this customer is in this cell right now?
Cognition	Interpret signals and predict intent and next action	LLMs, causal inference engines, knowledge graphs	What does this signal pattern mean, and what will this customer need next?
Actuation	Deliver personalized interventions across devices	Orchestration APIs, MCP, AR/VR, dynamic pricing	What response should we trigger, on which device, at what moment?
Emotion	Calibrate the emotional register of all interventions	Sentiment analysis, affective computing, voice tonality	What is the emotional state of this customer, and how should it shape our response?

The Emotion Layer is the most important addition. The original Matrix treated customer interactions as primarily rational transactions. The research literature on customer experience has consistently demonstrated that emotional memory — how customers feel after an interaction — is a stronger predictor of loyalty, word-of-mouth behavior, and lifetime value than satisfaction with the rational outcome of the interaction. A customer who reaches the right resolution after an exhausting, frustrating process has the same rational outcome as a customer who reached the same resolution quickly and pleasantly. Their emotional residue, and therefore their future behavior, will be dramatically different.

> ***"The Matrix 2.0 treats emotion not as a soft variable but as the primary output metric of customer experience management."***

The 15 Lifecycle Stages in the Sensor Economy

The 15 stages of the CxC Matrix remain the backbone of the 2.0 framework, but each has been reimagined for the Customer Sensor Mesh context:

Stage	Traditional Meaning	Customer Sensor Enhancement
1. Awareness	Customer discovers the brand	Includes algorithmic discovery by AI agents; machine-readable brand signals
2. Information	Customer researches options	Encompasses AI-mediated comparison; structured data feeds for agent evaluation
3. Identification	Customer self-identifies to brand	Biometric and behavioral authentication; persistent digital identity management
4. Selection	Customer chooses a product/service	AI recommendation systems; choice architecture optimized for automated agents
5. Negotiation	Customer negotiates terms	Machine-speed negotiation between AI agents; dynamic value exchange protocols
6. Contract	Customer formalizes agreement	Smart contracts; programmable terms; autonomous compliance verification
7. Logistics	Delivery is arranged	Predictive positioning; autonomous routing; just-in-time fulfillment
8. Delivery	Product/service is delivered	Physical, digital, and synthetic fulfillment; multi-reality delivery confirmation
9. Acceptance	Customer confirms receipt and satisfaction	Automated quality verification; biometric confirmation; AI outcome assessment

Stage	Traditional Meaning	Customer Sensor Enhancement
10. Collection	Payment is processed	Cryptocurrency, tokenized loyalty, micro-payments; value-exchange optimization
11. Use	Customer uses the product/service	Embedded sensor monitoring; predictive performance management; usage coaching
12. Care/Support	Customer needs help	Anticipatory service dispatch; predictive maintenance; zero-friction resolution
13. Repair	Customer reports a problem	Self-healing products; remote diagnostics; autonomous repair scheduling
14. Disposal	Customer lifecycle ends	Circular economy integration; sustainable disposition; lifecycle value recovery
15. Community	Customer becomes an advocate	Algorithmic advocacy; tokenized referral; AI-mediated trust network participation

The VMAO Cycle: Visualize, Monetize, Analyze, Optimize

The VMAO cycle is the operating process of the CxC Matrix — the continuous loop through which organizations transform customer data into operational intelligence and operational intelligence into business value. In the Customer Sensor economy, each step of the VMAO cycle is enhanced by AI capabilities that increase its speed, precision, and scope.

Visualize

In the original framework, visualization meant creating clear journey maps and channel diagrams that made customer experience visible to leadership teams across the customer's lifestages and across the company's channels. In the 3.0 framework, visualization extends to real-time dashboards that display live customer states across the full sensor mesh — showing not just where customers are in the lifecycle but what their current sensor signals indicate about their intent, emotional state, immediate needs, predicted path. and customer value 30, 60, 90, lifetime value predictions.

The most powerful visualizations in the Customer Sensor economy are predictive: they show not just where customers are now but where the current signal patterns suggest they will be in 2 minutes, 2 hours, and 2 weeks. These predictive visualizations allow operations teams to pre-position resources, pre-draft responses, and pre-optimize pathways before customers consciously form their next request.

Monetize

Monetization in the Matrix 3.0 framework operates at a new level of granularity. Each interaction slot — macro, micro, nano, and quantum — is assigned an economic value based on its contribution to customer lifetime value, its cost to serve, and its role in the customer's probability trajectory toward higher-value lifecycle stages.

The key innovation of the Customer Sensor era is the ability to monetize passive signals as well as active interactions. A customer's device uploading usage data generates economic value by improving prediction accuracy. A customer's wearable transmitting health data generates economic value by enabling anticipatory service. A customer's vehicle broadcasting maintenance telemetry generates economic value by creating proactive service opportunities. In each case, the customer's contribution to the company's data infrastructure is a form of value exchange that can and should be reflected in the economic model.

Analyze

Analysis in the Customer Sensor Mesh framework is driven by causal AI rather than correlational analytics. The critical question shifts from "what happened?" to "what caused what to happen, and what would cause something different?" This distinction matters enormously in the design of automated decision systems: a system trained on correlational data will replicate historical patterns, including historical biases and suboptimal outcomes. A system trained on causal models can identify the true drivers of customer behavior and optimize for changes that will produce genuinely better outcomes.

Optimize

Optimization in the 3.0 framework is continuous rather than periodic. The original VMAO cycle was designed to operate on a quarterly or annual review cadence — teams would analyze performance data, identify opportunities, design improvements, and implement them in the next cycle. The Customer Sensor Mesh infrastructure operates in milliseconds, and the optimization loop must match. Reinforcement learning agents monitor outcomes in real time, test micro-variations in treatment protocols, and continuously update the parameters of each Matrix cell based on observed performance.

The New Slot Taxonomy: Macro, Micro, Nano, and Quantum

One of the most important innovations of the CxC Matrix 3.0 is the expansion of container's "slots" concept — the unit of customer interaction — from a single level to four levels of granularity:

- Macro-slots: Components embedded in traditional customer touchpoints — a section of a web page, a prompt or offer in a phone script or service call, a greeting in a store or a closing message when handing product to customer during an in-store transaction. Measured in minutes. Planned at the campaign or journey level.
- Micro-slots: Brief moments of attention within a touchpoint — the few seconds a customer's gaze rests on a product image, the 300 milliseconds between a prompt appearing and a customer beginning to engage with it. Measured in seconds. Managed by interaction design.
- Nano-slots: Subconscious reactions measurable only through biometric sensors — the slight increase in skin conductance when a price is presented, the micro-expression of confusion when an interface is unclear, the brief drop in heart rate variability that signals cognitive load. Measured in milliseconds. Managed by affective computing systems.
- Quantum-slots: Predictive opportunities that exist before conscious awareness — the window of optimal receptivity that behavioral models predict

will occur based on time of day, recent activity patterns, and historical response data. Measured in probability distributions across time windows. Managed by predictive AI.

AI Prompt Library: CxC Matrix 3.0 Analysis

Prompt for Experience Analysts: "Analyze our customer journey for [product/service category]. Identify all micro-slots where customers show hesitation (dwell time >3 seconds or cursor pause >2 seconds). For each micro-slot, calculate the conversion impact if we reduce cognitive load by 20%. Recommend specific UX changes and predict ROI with confidence intervals. Then identify all nano-slots where biometric signals would indicate a different response pattern than the behavioral data suggests — these represent opportunities where the rational experience and the emotional experience are misaligned."

Hypothetical Case Study: nL'Oréal's Cognitive Beauty Matrix

In 2029, nL'Oréal deployed what internal teams called the Cognitive Beauty Matrix — a Customer Sensor Mesh platform that integrated their digital commerce infrastructure with a network of smart mirrors in retail partner locations, a mobile app with AI-powered skin analysis, and a customer permission program that allowed willing participants to share biometric skin health data in exchange for personalized product recommendations and loyalty rewards.

The system operated across all four cognitive processing layers. At the Perception Layer, smart mirrors captured facial biometric data that the system analyzed for skin type, tone, hydration level, and visible signs of specific concerns. At the Cognition Layer, an LLM-based recommendation engine interpreted this data in conjunction with the customer's purchase history, expressed preferences, social network commentary and behavior, and demographic context to generate personalized product recommendations with predictive efficacy scoring. At the Actuation Layer, the recommendations were delivered through the mirror interface, the mobile app, and AI-personalized email sequences, and message threads. At the Emotion Layer, the system monitored engagement signals — time spent examining recommendations, facial expressions of interest or skepticism, vocal inflection during in-store consultations — and adjusted the tone, depth, and format of future communications accordingly.

The results demonstrated the compounding advantages of multi-layer sensor integration. Customers with active smart mirror profiles showed 47% higher average order values than comparable non-enrolled customers. First-year churn rates in the enrolled segment were 31% lower. The program generated a net promoter score 28 points higher than the brand average — driven primarily by customers' perception that the brand "understood them" in ways that felt genuinely personal rather than algorithmically produced. (Hypothetical scenario discussed in blend of workshops not related to L'Oreal nor competitors)

Part One: The 15 Stages — A Complete Operational Guide

Two truths define CxC Matrix management in the age of AI, and you need both simultaneously. The reassuring truth: the fundamentals of what makes a great customer experience have not changed and will not change. Customers want to feel known. They want their needs met efficiently and with some degree of warmth. They want certainty. They want to feel that the company they chose values the relationship as much as they value the product. None of that is altered by

AI. If anything, AI raises the stakes — because it raises the baseline expectation for how well a company should be able to know and serve each individual customer.

The challenging truth: the operational requirements for delivering great customer experience have changed dramatically, and they will keep changing faster than most organizations are currently prepared to manage. The channels multiply. The data volume explodes. The customer's synthetic representation starts making decisions before the human customer is even aware. The pace of interaction compresses from days to seconds. The competitive bar rises continuously, set by whoever moved fastest last quarter.

> ***"The CxC Matrix is not a historical artifact. It was built for exactly this environment — complex, multi-channel, data-rich, AI-enhanced, and relentlessly customer-centric. Its 90 cells are not a limitation. They are a forcing function."***

Every cell in the matrix that is managed well is a competitive advantage. Every cell left unmanaged is a gap a competitor can walk through. The following stage-by-stage analysis applies this discipline with the precision the sensor economy demands.

The Competitor Is Always Present

At every stage, your customer is simultaneously being pursued by competitors who know the same lifecycle model you do and are designing their interventions accordingly. Stages 1 through 6 — Awareness through Contract — carry the highest defection risk because the customer has not yet fully committed. A well-designed CxC Matrix is not just a customer satisfaction tool. It is a competitive defense system, engineered to advance the customer through each stage faster, more confidently, and with greater certainty than any alternative can offer.

STAGE 1 — *The Moment the Clock Starts — and It May Start Without You*

Awareness

Every customer relationship begins with a spark. But what has fundamentally changed is this: that spark is increasingly lit not by your marketing department, but by the world around your customer — and increasingly by AI systems operating quietly in the background of their lives. A finance manager reads about a competitor's data breach and suddenly prioritizes the cybersecurity solution their IT team has been requesting. A college student stumbles across a 47-second video of perfectly crispy Brussels sprouts in an air fryer and a product category they'd never considered becomes an immediate want. These are awareness stories we recognize.

But consider the Awareness story we are entering now. A refrigerator camera captures a bottle of orange juice running low and cross-references it against health monitoring data suggesting increased Vitamin C consumption this week — awareness of a need, created autonomously. A smart power meter registers that a twelve-year-old washing machine is drawing 40% more electricity than its rated consumption, a signature pattern predicting imminent motor failure — awareness of a problem created before the problem occurs. A friend posts a selfie and an AI identifies a discontinued product with a safety advisory in the background of the photograph — awareness delivered from someone else's image.

CxC Matrix 3.0 + AI: *Awareness is no longer exclusively a marketing function. It is increasingly a data, AI, and product intelligence function. The question is not just "where are we advertising?" — it is "what signals in our customers' environments indicate an emerging need, and how quickly can we surface relevant Awareness in a way that feels helpful rather than intrusive?" Companies that answer that question well are present at the moment of need creation. Everyone else arrives three weeks later, after the customer has already formed a shortlist.*

STAGE 2 — *The Research Gauntlet, Now With an AI Co-Pilot*

Information

The need has been identified. Now the customer goes looking for answers. But "looking" in 2030 looks nothing like it did five years ago — and is about to look nothing like it does today. The Information stage is where a customer tries to understand how best to meet their need by identifying potential solutions that fit their specific context. Not just "what solves this problem" but "what solves this problem for me, in my situation, with my constraints, at this moment." That context is rich and multi-dimensional: urgency, budget, environmental fit, technical confidence, household dynamics, sustainability preferences, social context.

In the AI era, behavioral data, situation analysis, device ecosystem signals, purchase history, search patterns, and inferred preferences assemble a remarkably accurate picture of that context automatically — and use it to surface information genuinely fitted to this specific person. More than 80% of consumers research online before any significant purchase, consulting sources your company does not control. They are asking AI assistants that synthesize multiple sources into a single conversational answer. They are reading forum threads where your brand's reputation is being shaped by people you have never spoken to.

CxC Matrix 3.0 + AI: *Your content must be machine-readable — structured for AI retrieval, accurate in third-party databases, present in the formats where AI assistants source their answers. If a customer asks an AI assistant to help them research options in your category and your product is not accurately represented, you do not lose a consideration — you never enter one. Companies that provide genuinely useful, contextually intelligent information at Stage 2 build trust that no competitor's marketing budget can easily undo.*

STAGE 3 — *The Cut List, Curated by Intelligence*

Identification

Research generates options. Identification narrows them. And the criteria driving that narrowing are more complex, more personal, and more AI-legible than most companies design for. Identification includes both the preferences the customer can articulate and the ones they cannot. The customer knows they want something under $400. They may not consciously know that they consistently choose products with minimal visual complexity — but their purchase history shows it. Expert AI identification works by integrating stated preferences, inferred preferences, behavioral signals, environmental constraints, and contextual requirements — filtering the universe of options to a genuinely fitted shortlist.

A spatial AI cross-references product dimensions against the customer's known space configuration, eliminating options that physically don't fit. A compatibility AI checks the product against every other device in the customer's ecosystem, flagging integration gaps. A social proof AI weights options based on the specific peer groups this customer actually trusts — not aggregate star ratings, but the ratings of people whose taste and situation most closely matches theirs. This is AI working as a genuine customer advocate: narrowing choices in ways that respect the full complexity of what "right for this person" actually means.

CxC Matrix 3.0 + AI: *The Identification stage in its AI-enhanced form is not a filter. It is a curation — an intelligent narrowing that respects the full complexity of what "right for this customer" actually means. And at this stage, your competitor is doing the same work. The organization whose AI curation is most accurate, most contextually relevant, and most trustworthy wins the shortlist. Winning the shortlist is winning the stage.*

STAGE 4 — *The Arena, Equipped With Every Advantage*

Selection

The customer has a shortlist. Now they are comparing finalists. And AI is transforming Selection from a passive evaluation into an active, dynamic, personalized experience. An AI-powered Selection experience knows this customer is standing near a retail location with three of their shortlisted products in stock for immediate inspection. It knows the customer has an urgent timeline because the old appliance failed three days ago, which changes option weighting dramatically — in-stock availability and same-day pickup move up; features requiring a two-week wait move down. It knows a competing product is on sale this week at a nearby retailer.

Selection in the AI era also means prescriptive configuration — not just "here's what it costs" but "here's the optimal bundle for your situation," presented before the customer has asked for it. Financing options are dynamically surfaced. Upcoming release dates for next-generation models are flagged transparently — because a customer who buys the current model three weeks before a significant upgrade announcement becomes a dissatisfied customer, and an AI that surfaces that information proactively becomes a trusted advisor. Tutorial and training resources are previewed before purchase — because a customer who can see that onboarding is simple and guided is more confident buying than one who wonders if they'll figure it out.

CxC Matrix 3.0 + AI: *The Selection stage presents not just a product but the totality of a solution — product, configuration, services, financing, support resources, environmental fit, and timing — assembled specifically for this customer's complete situation. That is categorically different from a product page with a star rating and an "add to cart" button. And it wins at a categorically different rate.*

STAGE 5 — *Expert Advocacy — Now on the Customer's Side*

Negotiation

The customer has mentally selected. Now comes negotiation — and in the AI era, the customer is no longer negotiating alone or underprepared. For most of commercial history, negotiation was asymmetric. The seller knew their margin, their inventory position, their competitive situation, their authority to discount, and the full range of what was on the table. The buyer knew their budget and their desire. The seller almost always had the information advantage. That asymmetry is being dismantled — not gradually but rapidly.

AI negotiation agents operating on behalf of buyers now arrive with information parity: real-time market pricing across competitors, historical price trend data, knowledge of the seller's typical discount patterns, understanding of which terms are genuinely fixed versus which are negotiating positions, and the patience and consistency no human buyer can maintain under pressure. More profoundly, everything is on the table — price, warranty terms, service level agreements, delivery timing, bundle configurations, trade-in credit, training access, data privacy terms, return conditions, and performance guarantees. The companies that win in AI-mediated negotiation make their genuine value so clear, their terms so transparent, and their configured solutions so well-fitted that the agent concludes — accurately — that this is the best available deal.

CxC 3.0 + AI: *Stage 5 carries CRITICAL defection risk. A customer who has mentally selected you but encounters opacity, friction, or apparent misalignment in negotiation is a customer an attentive competitor can still intercept. Design the negotiation experience as a demonstration of what partnership with you will feel like — and close the deal before the competitor's follow-up arrives.*

STAGE 6 — *The Sacred Moment of Commitment*

Contract

The deal is made. The customer clicks "buy," signs the agreement, submits the purchase order. This should be the easiest stage in the entire journey — pure friction removal — and yet nearly 70% of online shopping carts are abandoned because something in the Contract stage created doubt or difficulty. An unexpected shipping cost. A mandatory account creation. A payment form that didn't accept the customer's preferred method. A terms scroll that implied something the customer hadn't bargained for.

These are not conversion optimization problems. They are Contract stage design failures with measurable revenue costs. Leading organizations treat Contract as sacred: one-click purchase where possible, every payment method the customer might prefer, e-signature for anything requiring a signature, auto-fill everything the system already knows, trust signals placed precisely where doubt tends to emerge. The economic calculation is among the simplest in the entire matrix — every friction point you remove at Stage 6 converts directly to revenue from customers who had already decided to buy. You are not persuading them. You are simply getting out of your own way.

CxC Matrix 3.0 + AI: *The buyer's remorse window opens the moment the contract is signed. A proactive confirmation message — warm, specific, and celebratory — delivered within minutes of commitment is the most cost-effective post-sale investment your organization can make. It closes the window before a competitor's remarketing ad finds it.*

STAGE 7 — *Time, Proximity, and the Experience of Waiting*

Logistics

Logistics has been revolutionized by Amazon and now needs to be rethought again — because what's being delivered, when the benefit starts, and how the customer measures "arrival" are all more complex than a tracking number suggests. For a physical product, delivery means the product reaches the customer's door. But when does the benefit start? For software, benefit starts at download — potentially seconds after purchase. For a service subscription, benefit starts at account activation. For a product requiring professional installation, benefit doesn't start until a certified installer completes their work — which might be two weeks after the box arrives.

The CxC Matrix should map logistics against benefit-start timing, not just delivery-completion timing, because the customer's experience of waiting is measured against when they expected to begin receiving value. Proximity is increasingly a logistics variable — not just "when will it arrive" but "where is it right now and how does that change my options?" A customer who discovers that three units are in a store 2.3 miles away may choose a different logistics path than initially selected — if your system offers that visibility in real time. First-time versus repeat buyer logistics design is another dimension most companies flatten inappropriately.

CxC Matrix 3.0 + AI: *AI-optimized logistics means the system knows this customer's schedule, delivery history, and preferences — and proactively selects the option most likely to satisfy them before they need to think about it. The logistics experience is a trust event. Manage it as one.*

STAGE 8 — *From Bare Bones to White Glove — and Everything Between*

Delivery

The product arrives. The service begins. This is the first moment the customer encounters your company through something other than a screen, and the quality of that moment is your first opportunity to confirm that their decision was right. The delivery experience exists on a spectrum, and AI can now configure that spectrum dynamically based on what each customer's situation calls for. At the bare-bones end: fast, reliable, frictionless — product arrives when promised, in good condition, with clear next steps. For repeat buyers of familiar products, elegance is speed and accuracy, not ceremony.

At the white-glove, concierge end: the delivery team calls forty-eight hours ahead to confirm timing, arrives within a two-hour window, removes and disposes of the old product responsibly, installs the new one, tests it to full operation, walks the customer through key features in person, and does not leave until the customer confirms they are comfortable. For high-value purchases, first-time buyers, elderly customers, or products with meaningful installation complexity, white-glove delivery is not a luxury upsell — it is the experience that prevents the onboarding failures that drive early returns and negative reviews. Nine in ten customers believe companies should "know their needs" and deliver immediate value from the first moment of contact.

CxC Matrix 3.0 + AI: *The delivery stage is the opening act of the customer's ownership experience. A poor delivery — damaged packaging, missed window, no communication — can undo every investment made in Stages 1 through 7. An exceptional delivery — personal, precise, welcoming — can create the kind of first impression that drives Stage 15 Community advocacy before the customer has even tried the product.*

STAGE 9 — *The Verdict — and the Broadcast*

Acceptance

The customer has the product. Now they are deciding whether it lives up to the promise. This is the Acceptance stage — the unboxing, the setup, the first use, the moment of truth that determines whether the gap between expectation and reality closes or widens. The physical ritual of acceptance has been transformed by social media into a performance. Unboxing videos collectively generate billions of views annually. The moment of opening a package is now frequently a broadcast — shared with followers, friends, and communities who are simultaneously experiencing the product vicariously and forming opinions about it.

Your packaging, presentation, and first-impression contents are not just functional — they are potentially broadcast content, and they should be designed with that reality in mind. The Acceptance stage is one of the highest-shareability moments in the entire customer lifecycle. Companies that design acceptance experiences with shareability as an explicit objective — packaging that photographs beautifully, first-use moments that generate genuine delight, personal touches worth commenting on — are creating marketing content at the customer's hands, at the customer's initiative, with a credibility no paid placement can match. Proper onboarding at this stage improves long-term product usage by 55% and dramatically increases retention.

CxC Matrix 3.0 + AI: *The acceptance experience determines how the customer enters Stage 11 Use. A customer who accepted the product with delight, shared it with their network, and completed their onboarding with confidence is a categorically different future customer than one who struggled with setup, found the product underwhelming, and told no one.*

STAGE 10 — *Every Currency, Every Configuration*

Payment / Collection

Money changes hands. And today, "money" is a more creative concept than it has ever been. Nearly one in five Americans recently used buy-now-pay-later services, reflecting a fundamental shift in how customers prefer to align payment timing with value realization. Subscription models have multiplied to the point where the average consumer has more recurring charges than they can name from memory. Loyalty points as full or partial currency — made mainstream by Starbucks and now deployed across airlines, hotels, credit card programs, and expanding retail sectors.

The truly creative payment frontier involves configurations most companies

A customer who participates in a case study, a beta program, or a product review process receives credit against their purchase — a transaction that generates marketing value and customer investment simultaneously. Community contribution credit: platforms that reward meaningful community participation — thoughtful reviews, tutorial content, peer support — with purchasing credit are turning Stage 15 Community behavior into Stage 10 payment currency, creating a virtuous cycle that compounds. In the Customer Sensor economy, payment also includes data-value exchange: customers who grant higher-tier permission levels receive economic benefit in the form of personalized pricing, exclusive offers, and enhanced service.

CxC MTRIX 3.0 + AI: *Do your payment options match your customers' actual preferences, or your company's operational convenience? The gap between those two things is a measurable source of friction, abandoned purchases, and preventable churn. Every payment method you don't accept is a gate you've installed in your own conversion funnel.*

STAGE 11 — *The Longest Stage — Across All Four Domains*

Use

Here is the paradox at the heart of most customer experience programs: the stage that spans the longest period of the customer relationship receives the least deliberate design attention. Marketing obsesses over Awareness. Sales owns Contract. Operations owns Delivery. And then the customer starts actually using the product for months or years, and the organization's attention largely moves on to the next new customer. This is not just backwards — in the era of connected products, it is a significant and calculable missed revenue opportunity.

Use must now be understood across all four customer domains simultaneously, because use is no longer a single-mode experience. In the physical domain, use is the customer's embodied interaction with the product. In the digital domain, use generates a continuous stream of behavioral data — how often, how long, which features, in what sequence — that reveals usage drop-offs predicting churn weeks before the customer consciously decides to leave. Companies using predictive analytics on usage data have documented up to 25% revenue growth from pre-empting churn. In the synthetic domain, the customer's AI representation may be using the product on their behalf autonomously and continuously, with the human customer reviewing outcomes rather than directing individual actions.

CxC Matrix 3.0 + AI: *Autonomous use and autonomous benefit — products that deliver value without requiring active human operation — represent the frontier of Stage 11. The critical design challenge: how do you ensure the customer knows the value they are receiving from something operating invisibly on their behalf? Value visibility is not a communication challenge. It is an experience design requirement.*

STAGE 12 — *Self-Healing, Self-Enhancing, Always On*

Care and Support

The customer needs help. How your company responds determines more about long-term loyalty than almost anything else in the journey. Ninety percent of customers say immediate response is important. "Immediate" now means now — and AI-powered support available 24 hours a day across every channel is rapidly making instant response the standard expectation rather than a premium differentiator. By 2028, AI handles the first layer of customer interaction for the majority of support contacts across many industries — routing, triaging, resolving standard issues, providing contextually relevant guidance — with seamless escalation to human agents for complex or emotional situations.

But the Care stage is evolving beyond reactive AI support into something more profound: self-healing and self-enhancing products that identify, diagnose, and resolve issues before the customer experiences them as problems. A software platform that detects an impending database performance issue and automatically scales resources before the user experiences slowdown. A connected medical device that identifies a calibration drift and self-corrects while notifying the care team. A home HVAC system that diagnoses a developing refrigerant issue, schedules a service appointment, and orders the required parts — all before the homeowner's home gets warm on a July afternoon. These are not incremental improvements to customer support. They are a redefinition of what support means.

CxC Matrix 3.0 + AI: *The support function that helps a customer unlock a feature they didn't know existed is generating loyalty value at the cost of a single interaction. In a world of high switching costs but declining switching friction, great support at Stage 12 is one of the most cost-effective competitive moats available.*

STAGE 13 — *Preventive, Heroic, and Intimate*

Repair

Something went wrong. Or — in the AI-enhanced world — something was about to go wrong, and your system caught it first. Repair is the most intimate stage in the entire customer journey. It is the moment of maximum vulnerability — the customer is disappointed, possibly frustrated, possibly facing real consequences of a failure in their life or business. How your company shows up in that moment is the purest expression of what your brand actually values, stripped of all marketing language.

The best repair experiences are preventive — the failure is detected before it occurs, the maintenance is scheduled before it becomes urgent, and the customer's experience is that the product took care of itself with minimal disruption. When prevention fails and a genuine repair situation occurs, the standard should be nothing less than hero-level support — regardless of cause. Whether the failure was a product defect, a service gap, an environmental factor, or the customer's own unintended misuse: the customer standing in front of a broken thing they paid for deserves advocacy, not interrogation. Ritz-Carlton employees are authorized to spend up to $2,000 per guest to resolve any problem without manager approval.

CxC Matrix 3.0 + AI: *A company that performs heroically in a repair moment often emerges with a stronger customer relationship than existed before the failure. Repair is rich with customer engagement potential. The customer who experiences extraordinary recovery does not just stay — they tell people. Every channel in the matrix should have a defined repair presence. Especially Community.*

STAGE 14 — *End of Life — Beginning of Responsibility*

Disposal

Every product eventually reaches the end of its useful life. Every service contract eventually comes up for renewal or termination. Every relationship reaches a pivot point: deepen, transition, or end. The Disposal stage is where most companies fail their customers — and increasingly, fail the broader world — most visibly. The circular economy imperative has moved from sustainability preference to strategic requirement: customers, investors, and regulators increasingly expect organizations to design for responsible end-of-life from the beginning.

Refurbishment programs that accept trade-ins, restore products to certified condition, and resell them at accessible price points extend product life, reduce raw material demand, and create a new customer segment simultaneously. Take-back and recycling programs that make responsible disposal effortless — scheduled pickup, prepaid shipping labels, in-store drop-off — remove the guilt and inconvenience that cause customers to defer disposal indefinitely. The most creative disposal innovations engineer end-of-life into the product from the beginning: self-dissolving packaging, pod recycling programs as simple as the purchase itself, lease structures where the manufacturer retains ownership and responsibility for end-of-life.

CxC Matrix 3.0 + AI: *The Disposal stage, managed well, is not the end of the customer story. It is an expression of the company's values at the moment when the commercial incentive to impress has passed — and customers notice. Customers who experience a thoughtful, responsible disposal process are customers who return, refer, and advocate. Customers who are simply abandoned at end-of-life leave without saying goodbye — and say something on their way out.*

STAGE 15 — *The Social, Digital, Empathetic Platform That Feeds Everything Else*

Community

And now the stage that most companies underinvest in most dramatically. The stage that is simultaneously a marketing channel, a product development resource, a trust infrastructure, a social platform, and an expression of the company's relationship with the world beyond its direct customers. Community is where the customer's experience becomes public, permanent, and influential. Eighty-four percent of people trust online reviews as much as personal recommendations from friends. More than 75% of consumers read reviews before almost any significant purchase. Referrals from community advocates convert at 30% higher rates and carry 16% higher lifetime value than customers acquired through other channels.

But community today is more than reviews and referrals. It is a living library of use cases, configurations, creative applications, and expert advice generated by people who know the product more intimately than most of the company's employees. The most sophisticated community platforms bring together four layers: the social layer that connects customers with shared interests; the technological layer that integrates community with product and surfaces community expertise at relevant moments in the journey; the digital layer that extends community into the broader ecosystem where AI-curated content influences future customers' Stage 2 research; and the empathetic layer — the one most companies miss entirely — where community creates meaning, connection, and belonging that extends far beyond the product that catalyzed it.

CxC Matrix 3.0 + AI: *Companies that understand and invest in the empathetic layer of community are not just building customer loyalty. They are building something customers genuinely value in their own right. That is the deepest form of Customer Worthiness: not a company that sells well, but a community that people are genuinely glad to belong to.*

Part Two: The Six Channels — The Landscape of Customer Life

Fifteen stages. The complete arc of the customer relationship, from the first spark of awareness to the deepest form of advocacy. But stages alone do not give you the full picture. They tell you where the customer is in the relationship. They do not tell you where the customer is in the world — and that matters just as much.

> ***"Your customer exists in all six channels. You do not get to decide that. You do get to decide which channels you invest in, which you monitor, and which you leave unattended. Those are real strategic choices with real financial consequences — whether you made them deliberately or by default."***

The six channels are not a menu of distribution options your company selects from. They are the landscape of human life in which your customer is already living — and within which they will seek to fulfill every one of the 15 lifecycle stages, with or without your participation, using whatever resources they can find, in whatever channel is most convenient, available, and suited to their situation at that moment.

Abandonment Has a Cost

The six channels are not yours to create. They are yours to manage — or to abandon. And abandonment has a cost that is just as real as the cost of investment, even if it is harder to see on a balance sheet. The customer doesn't know or care which cells you have chosen to manage and which you have chosen to ignore. They experience the full channel landscape as a continuous, connected journey. A gap in your channel coverage is not a strategic distinction to them. It is simply an absence — filled by whoever showed up.

CHANNEL 1 | Geography

The Dimension That Sets All the Rules

Your customer lives somewhere. They experience the world from a specific physical location — a city, a neighborhood, a postal code, a timezone, a climate, a cultural context, a regulatory jurisdiction, a competitive landscape. That geography shapes everything about what they can access, what they expect, what they pay, and how they experience every other channel. Geography is the invisible envelope that contains all the other channels and determines what is possible within each of them. A customer in rural Montana experiences the digital channel through infrastructure constraints that a customer in Manhattan doesn't face. A customer in Germany experiences the third-party channel through regulatory frameworks — GDPR, product liability law, marketplace regulations — that a customer in Brazil navigates differently.

Companies manage geography through coverage decisions — where they operate, where they ship, which markets they serve — and through localization decisions — how they adapt pricing, product configuration, marketing messaging, and service delivery to the specific context of each geography. In the AI era, geography has become dynamic rather than static. Real-time location signals, geofencing, proximity-based offers, and location-aware service configuration mean that geography is now an active input into every interaction — not a background variable set when the customer account was created. The customer walking past your store right now is in a different geographic context than the same customer browsing your website from their couch at home, and an AI-powered experience can recognize and respond to that difference in real time.

Channel Economics: *Geography determines cost-to-serve in ways no other variable matches. Logistics costs, regulatory compliance, local marketing, support staffing, and competitive pricing pressure all vary by geography — making it the foundation of any honest customer lifetime value calculation. A customer in a high-cost-to-serve geography with identical purchase behavior represents meaningfully different economic value — and the CxC Matrix 3.0 forces that geography-adjusted calculation.*

CHANNEL 2 | Digital

The Channel the Customer Never Closes

Your customer has a smartphone. Almost certainly, multiple screens, multiple accounts, multiple digital identities across multiple platforms, and a continuous ambient connection to the digital world that is never fully switched off. They wake up with a screen and fall asleep with one. The digital channel is the first place most customers go to meet any information need, consider any purchase, seek any support, or share any experience — across every one of the 15 lifecycle stages. An AI assistant that researches products overnight while the customer sleeps, compares options across dozens of sources, and presents a synthesized recommendation by morning is using the digital channel on the customer's behalf at Stages 2 and 3 without any active customer effort.

Companies that have not invested in digital channel presence across multiple lifecycle stages are not simply underperforming in that channel. They are absent from the primary arena in which modern customer decision-making occurs — and their absence is filled by competitors, third-party sources, and AI systems that may or may not represent their brand accurately. The digital channel also has the highest measurability of any channel in the matrix. Every interaction generates data. Every click, query, scroll, conversion, and departure is trackable, analyzable, and actionable. This makes the digital channel the most powerful laboratory in the CxC Matrix 3.0 for testing, optimizing, and calculating the return on every interaction.

Channel Economics: *Digital has the lowest marginal cost per interaction at scale and the highest potential for AI-driven personalization — making it the channel with the highest theoretical ROI for customer experience investment. It also has the highest noise-to-signal ratio and the most intense competition for customer attention. The companies winning in digital are not the ones spending the most. They are the ones measuring the most precisely and optimizing the most continuously.*

CHANNEL 3 | Location

Physical Space as a Channel Choice — Not a Default

Your customer has a body. They move through physical space. They visit stores, offices, branches, kiosks, and events. And despite decades of predictions about the irrelevance of physical presence in a digital world, customers continue to value — and often prefer — physical interaction for specific lifecycle stages and specific types of decisions. The Location channel is every physical space where your company and your customer can meet in the real world — but it also includes the customer's own physical environment, their home, office, or vehicle, as an increasingly active channel through which connected products and embedded AI services deliver ongoing value.

Here is the critical reframe for the Location channel: it is a choice the customer makes, not a default. A customer who visits your physical location at Stage 4 — Selection — has chosen to invest their time, transportation, and physical presence because they believe the physical channel will give them something the digital channel cannot: the ability to touch, evaluate, compare, and experience the product in person. If your physical location doesn't deliver meaningfully superior insight or experience to what the digital channel provides, the customer's investment in that visit is not justified — and they will remember that the next time they are deciding whether to visit or just buy online.

Channel Economics: *Physical has the highest cost-per-interaction of any channel and the highest potential for emotional impact and trust formation. A meaningful face-to-face interaction at the right lifecycle stage can create loyalty that no digital touchpoint can replicate. But irrelevant, understaffed, or poorly designed physical interactions have a proportionally higher negative impact — the customer invested time, not just attention, and they expect a return on that investment.*

CHANNEL 4 | Third Party

The Channel You Don't Own But Can't Ignore

Your customer's relationship with your brand doesn't exist in a vacuum. It exists inside an ecosystem of third parties: marketplace platforms, review sites, comparison engines, industry publications, social media platforms, influencer networks, partner integrations, reseller channels, regulatory bodies, and increasingly, AI systems that aggregate and synthesize information from all of these sources into a single recommendation. The Third-Party channel is every touchpoint where your brand, product, or service is represented, evaluated, or discussed by parties other than your company — and where your customer encounters that representation as part of their lifecycle journey.

In Stage 2 — Information — more than 70% of customers consult at least one third-party source during their research. In Stage 13 — Repair — a dissatisfied customer's community post or review may be read by thousands of prospective customers navigating their own Stage 2. The Third-Party channel is where your brand's reputation is publicly maintained, publicly challenged, and publicly resolved — and where the interactions of your existing customers directly shape the decisions of your future ones. AI has fundamentally changed the dynamics of the third-party channel by becoming the primary curator of third-party information.

Channel Economics: *Third-party channel management has a unique economics: the cost is primarily reputational infrastructure — review management, media relations, partner program management, regulatory compliance — rather than direct per-interaction cost. But the leverage is extraordinary. A single viral negative review can generate $10M+ in brand damage. A single strategic partnership integration can open a new market segment. The ROI on proactive third-party channel management compounds asymmetrically.*

CHANNEL 5 | One-on-One

The Channel That Creates the Relationships Nothing Else Can

Every other channel scales through efficiency. The One-on-One channel scales through depth. This is the channel of the individual relationship — the account manager who knows their customer's business better than the customer's own colleagues, the service technician who has been maintaining the same equipment for fifteen years and knows its quirks by sound, the financial advisor who has guided a client through three market cycles, a divorce, and two business partnerships. These relationships are not replicable at scale. They are not scalable in the way that a website or an email sequence is scalable. And that is precisely what makes them valuable.

AI does not replace the One-on-One channel. It enables the human beings operating within it to perform at a level previously possible only for the most gifted and experienced practitioners. An account manager supported by an AI system that surfaces real-time customer context, predicts emerging needs, flags early warning signals of dissatisfaction, and recommends the most effective intervention for each situation can manage relationships at a depth and quality that would require years of experience to achieve without AI augmentation. In the Customer Sensor era, the One-on-One channel's role is evolving: less about information transfer, which AI handles more efficiently, and more about emotional intelligence, complex judgment, and the irreplaceable experience of feeling genuinely seen and understood by another human being.

Channel Economics: *The One-on-One channel carries the highest cost-per-interaction of any channel. It also carries the highest potential lifetime value per customer. The economic question is precision: which customers and which lifecycle stages genuinely require one-on-one investment to achieve their maximum value potential? The CxC Matrix 3.0 answers that question systematically — and AI's ability to predict which interactions will create the most value guides that resource allocation.*

CHANNEL 6 | Community

The Channel That Belongs to Your Customers — Not to You

Community is the only channel in the CxC Matrix that your customers own more than you do. It is the channel of peer relationships, shared experience, public reputation, and collective knowledge. It includes formal community platforms — forums, user groups, certified partner networks, customer advisory boards — and informal community spaces — social media conversations, review platforms, industry events, word-of-mouth networks. Most importantly, it includes the organic, unmediated conversations about your brand that happen without your involvement, in spaces you may not even monitor.

The Community channel operates across every lifecycle stage: potential customers consult it at Stage 2 for social proof, at Stage 4 for comparison evidence, at Stage 12 and 13 for peer support when things go wrong. Existing customers contribute to it at Stage 15 when they have something to say — positive or negative. The most powerful dynamic in the Community channel is the self-reinforcing cycle between Stage 11 Use quality and Stage 15 Community contribution: customers who experience genuine value in their use become authentic advocates; their advocacy attracts new customers who enter with appropriately calibrated expectations; those customers, in turn, experience genuine value; and the cycle strengthens.

Channel Economics: *Community has unique economics: it is simultaneously your lowest-cost acquisition channel (referred customers acquire at a fraction of paid channel costs) and your highest-value retention infrastructure (community members churn at significantly lower rates than isolated customers). The investment required to build and sustain genuine community — not managed brand presence, but real community — is substantial. The return is compounding and largely irreversible as a competitive advantage once established.*

The Economics Hidden in Every Cell

A support chat at Stage 12 in the digital channel might cost $4 to deliver through an AI-assisted system. If it resolves the customer's issue completely and generates a follow-up score that predicts continued subscription, it protects $840 in annual recurring revenue and contributes to a lifetime value calculation that justifies the next year of retention investment. That is a calculable return. A community forum post at Stage 15 — a detailed, enthusiastic review from a satisfied customer — might have required zero direct investment to generate. It influences twelve prospective customers during their Stage 2 research, converts three to Stage 3 consideration, and contributes to one final purchase with a projected lifetime value of $2,400. The framework for this calculation exists. The data exists. The AI to perform it at scale exists. What most companies are missing is the matrix structure that connects the interaction to the outcome to the lifetime value in a coherent, trackable chain.

The 90 Cells: Building the Performance Accountability Framework

Fifteen stages multiplied by six channels produces the 90 cells that define the CxC Matrix operational universe. Each cell is the intersection of a specific customer state (where they are in their relationship lifecycle) and a specific interaction environment (the channel through which they are currently engaging). Each cell has a distinct economic profile, a distinct set of likely customer needs, a distinct set of competitive risks, and a distinct set of AI capabilities that can optimize performance.

In the original CxC Matrix, each cell contained 9 treatment objectives: Identify, Recognize, Fulfill, Upgrade, Cross-Sell, Expand, Educate, Collect, and Generate Referrals. In the Matrix 2.0, each cell contains those same 9 objectives, now layered across 4 cognitive processing dimensions (Perception, Cognition, Actuation, Emotion), producing 810 discrete performance accountability points per interaction session. The VMAO cycle — Visualize, Monetize, Analyze, Optimize — drives continuous performance improvement across every one of those 810 points.

Cell Category	Stage Range	Primary Economic Objective	Primary AI Application
Acquisition cells	Stages 1-4 (Awareness through Selection)	Minimize cost per qualified prospect; maximize conversion to consideration	Predictive intent modeling; machine-aware content architecture
Conversion cells	Stages 5-7 (Negotiation through Logistics)	Maximize deal value; minimize time-to-close; reduce abandonment	Dynamic configuration; friction detection; commitment support
Activation cells	Stages 8-10 (Delivery through Payment)	Accelerate time-to-value; maximize first-experience quality	Acceptance experience design; payment optimization; early use coaching
Retention cells	Stages 11-12 (Use and Care/Support)	Maximize engagement depth; predict and prevent churn	Usage analytics; proactive care; anticipatory support
Recovery cells	Stages 13-14 (Repair	Convert failures to loyalty; manage end-	Predictive maintenance;

Cell Category	Stage Range	Primary Economic Objective	Primary AI Application
	through Disposal)	of-life as brand equity	emotional service design; circular economy
Growth cells	Stage 15 (Community)	Convert experience to advocacy; build self-reinforcing acquisition	Advocacy detection; referral timing; community intelligence

The CxC Matrix 3.0 AI Prompt Library: Complete Reference

The following AI prompt library provides tested, production-quality prompts for every major CxC Matrix analysis and design application. Each prompt is designed to produce actionable output that can be integrated directly into CxC Matrix 3.0 management processes. Prompts are organized by application type and include guidance on output interpretation.

Matrix Analysis Prompts

> **Full Matrix Performance Analysis**
>
> We are a [company description] with [X] customers across [Y] lifecycle stages and [Z] channels. I'm providing our CxC Matrix performance data including interaction volumes, conversion rates, customer satisfaction scores, and cost-per-interaction by cell. Please: (1) Identify the five cells with the largest gap between current performance and estimated optimal performance. (2) For each of these cells, diagnose the primary cause of underperformance — is it a sensing gap, an analytical gap, an actuation gap, or an

emotional calibration gap? (3) Estimate the revenue impact of closing each gap to industry benchmark performance. (4) Recommend the single highest-ROI improvement action for each cell and estimate the resources required. Present results in a prioritized action matrix sorted by estimated ROI.

Competitive Position Assessment

Analyze our competitive position in [market/category] from a Customer Sensor capability perspective. For our top [3-5] competitors: (1) Based on available public information, assess their Customer Sensor maturity across the five readiness dimensions: sensor infrastructure, AI analytical capability, automation level, permission architecture quality, and trust infrastructure. (2) Identify the two Customer Sensor capabilities where each competitor appears to have a meaningful advantage over us. (3) Identify the two Customer Sensor capabilities where we appear to have a meaningful advantage. (4) Based on technology investment trends and public announcements, forecast where each competitor is likely to be in 24 months. (5) Recommend the three capability investments that would most effectively protect our competitive position over the next 24 months.

Customer Segment Opportunity Identification

We have [X] customer segments with the following behavioral profiles: [paste segment data]. For each segment, using the CxC Matrix framework: (1) Identify which lifecycle stages each segment spends disproportionate time in (where dwell time is higher than expected for a healthy customer journey). (2) Identify which lifecycle stages show disproportionate churn risk for each segment. (3) Identify the three Customer Sensor capabilities that would have the highest impact on each segment's lifetime value. (4) Estimate the total available value improvement from Customer Sensor optimization for each segment. (5) Recommend the optimal sequence for Customer Sensor capability deployment given the relative segment value and implementation complexity.

Experience Design Prompts

Stage-Specific Experience Redesign

We need to redesign our customer experience at Stage [X: specify stage] × Channel [Y: specify channel]. Our current interaction design has the following characteristics: [describe current design]. Our performance metrics for this cell are: [provide metrics]. Please: (1) Identify the primary experience failure mode in the current design — is it premature state collapse, emotional monoculture, historical bias override, or symmetric empathy assumption? (2) Design an improved interaction protocol that addresses this failure mode using quantum empathy principles. (3) Specify the sensor data inputs required for the improved design and assess the data quality and availability for our organization. (4) Provide three specific intervention scripts optimized for the three most common customer states in this cell. (5) Define the success metrics for the redesigned experience and estimate the magnitude of improvement we should expect.

Permission Architecture Design

We want to build a permission architecture for our Customer Sensor program that balances data utility with customer trust. Our current data collection includes: [list current data types and uses]. We want to add the following new sensing capabilities: [list proposed additions]. Please: (1) Design a four-tier permission architecture appropriate for our customer base, defining the data types and use cases at each tier and the customer benefit proposition for each tier upgrade. (2) Design the consent flow for each tier transition — the specific communication, the opt-in mechanism, and the confirmation process. (3) Identify the three most sensitive data types in our proposed collection set and design specific privacy-preserving implementations for each. (4) Assess our proposal against GDPR, CCPA, and [other relevant framework] requirements and identify any gaps. (5) Estimate the proportion of our customer base likely to achieve each permission tier based on comparable implementations.

Digital Twin Model Specification

We want to build customer digital twin models for our Customer Sensor Schematic system. Our customer base has the following characteristics: [describe customer base]. Our available data sources include: [list data sources with update frequency and quality]. Please: (1) Design the five-layer digital twin architecture appropriate for our context — Identity Constellation, Intent Prediction, Emotional State, Value Optimization, and Action Orchestration layers. (2) For each layer, specify the data inputs, the modeling approach, the update frequency, and the accuracy validation method. (3) Identify the three behavioral signals that are most predictive of customer lifetime value change in our category and design the monitoring protocol for each. (4) Design the simulation environment specifications needed to test experience changes against our digital twin population. (5) Estimate the data infrastructure investment required to implement this architecture and the timeline to achieve reliable predictive accuracy.

Personalized Value Visibility Message

A customer [profile: describe relevant attributes] has been using our [product/service] for [time period]. Their usage data shows: [summarize key usage patterns]. Their satisfaction score is [score] and their churn risk assessment is [low/medium/high]. Draft a Value Exchange Statement message for this customer that: (1) Makes visible the specific value they have received from the relationship — quantify where possible (time saved, money saved, outcomes achieved). (2) Acknowledges any gaps where we have not fully delivered on our value proposition. (3) Previews the additional value they could receive by expanding their relationship (specific features, tiers, or capabilities relevant to their usage pattern). (4) Invites a specific next action that serves the customer's interests as clearly as it serves the business's interests. The message should be warm but not sycophantic, specific not generic, and no more than 150 words. Provide three tone variations: professional, conversational, and brief.

Quantum Empathy Service Recovery Script

A customer [profile] has experienced the following service failure: [describe failure]. Their interaction history with our organization includes: [summarize history]. Their current detected emotional state based on their recent contact behavior is: [describe]. They have [X] years as a customer and [describe relationship value]. Write a service recovery communication that: (1) Acknowledges all four likely emotional dimensions of their response to this failure (loyalty, betrayal, frustration, vulnerability) without assuming which is dominant. (2) Takes responsibility without being legally inadvisable. (3) Offers a specific, proportionate remedy calibrated to the relationship value and the severity of the failure. (4) Explains what we are doing to prevent this failure from recurring. (5) Leaves the customer feeling genuinely

> heard, genuinely respected, and genuinely confident that the relationship is worth maintaining. Write for [channel: email/voice script/chat].

CHAPTER THREE

Think Like a Customer 2035

Empathy at Quantum Scale

The Quantum Customer Paradox

The central paradox of customer experience in the 2030s is this: the more data we have about individual customers, the harder it becomes to understand them. This seems counterintuitive. With sensors monitoring every biometric signal, AI agents tracking every purchase, and behavioral models predicting every preference — shouldn't we know our customers better than ever?

The paradox resolves when you understand the quantum nature of modern customer psychology. A quantum system does not have a single definable state until it is observed. Before observation, it exists in a superposition of multiple possible states simultaneously. The modern customer is similar: before the moment of engagement, they simultaneously hold multiple, often contradictory motivations, preferences, and emotional states. They want to save money and they want the premium option. They want convenience and they want to feel valued as an individual. They want efficiency and they want the pleasure of exploring. They are, until the moment of interaction, in superposition.

The Customer Sensor Mesh system that attempts to collapse this superposition too early — that presents a single prediction as the definitive customer state before the customer has had the opportunity to crystallize their own preferences — will produce worse outcomes than a system that holds open the possibility space longer and allows the interaction itself to reveal the customer's true state.

> ***"The best customer experiences don't predict what customers want. They create the conditions in which customers discover what they want."***

From Touchpoints to Dynamic Customer Probability Clouds

Traditional CX frameworks treat customers as moving along linear or branching paths — a customer is "at" the Information stage, or "in" the Selection stage. This spatial metaphor implies a single location at a single moment in time. In the Customer Sensor economy, a more accurate metaphor is the probability cloud: at any given moment, a customer exists in a probabilistic distribution across multiple lifecycle stages simultaneously, with different weights in different channels and contexts.

A customer who browsed three competing products yesterday is simultaneously in the Information stage (they are still gathering data), the Selection stage (they are actively comparing), and the Negotiation stage (their comparison behavior signals that price sensitivity will be a factor). They are not "at" any one of these stages — they are in a superposition of all three, and the interaction that best serves them is one that honors the complexity of this multistage state rather than forcing a premature commitment to a single stage definition.

The Customer Sensor infrastructure makes this kind of probability-cloud thinking operationally practical. Instead of routing customers through predefined stage sequences, the Matrix 3.0 maintains a continuously updated probability distribution for each customer across all 15 lifecycle stages, all 6 channels, and all 4 cognitive processing layers. This distribution is updated in real time by new sensor signals and used to select the treatment protocol that maximizes expected lifetime value given the current state distribution.

Quantum Empathy: Understanding Superposition States

Empathy in the Customer Sensor era is not simply the ability to understand how a customer feels right now. It is the capacity to hold multiple, potentially contradictory understandings of how a customer feels simultaneously, and to respond in ways that honor that complexity rather than resolving it prematurely.

Consider a customer who has been with a company for seven years and has just experienced a significant service failure for the first time. Simultaneously, they feel: loyalty: seven years of positive experience; betrayal: the failure contradicts their established expectations; frustration: the immediate negative impact of the failure; and vulnerability: they trusted this company and it let them down. Any response that addresses only one of these emotional dimensions — a "we apologize for the inconvenience" that acknowledges frustration but ignores betrayal and vulnerability, or a "as a valued seven-year customer" that acknowledges loyalty but sidesteps the failure — will feel inadequate.

The Customer Sensor Mesh system that handles this interaction optimally is one that can simultaneously acknowledge all four emotional dimensions, calibrate the weight given to each based on behavioral signals, and deliver a response that demonstrates genuine understanding of the complexity of the customer's state. This is quantum empathy: holding and responding to the full superposition of a customer's emotional state rather than collapsing it to a single simplified descriptor.

Department-Specific Applications of Quantum Empathy

Quantum empathy is not a soft concept — it has specific operational implications for every function in a Customer Worthy organization:

Department	Traditional Empathy	Quantum Empathy in the Sensor Era
Sales	Understand the customer's stated needs	Model the full probability distribution of unstated needs, competing motivations, and decision triggers
Customer Service	Acknowledge the customer's frustration	Simultaneously address frustration, loyalty, vulnerability, and the systemic cause of the failure
Marketing	Segment customers by demographic or behavioral profile	Maintain individualized probability clouds for each customer across all relevant attributes
Product	Design for the median user need	Design for the distribution of user states, with adaptive

Department	Traditional Empathy	Quantum Empathy in the Sensor Era
		features that reconfigure for different probability profiles
Finance	Calculate customer lifetime value	Model the probability distribution of lifetime value scenarios given different intervention choices at each decision point
HR	Train employees to be customer-focused	Develop employees' capacity to hold and respond to multiple simultaneous customer states

The Quantum Empathy Operating Model

Quantum empathy is not a philosophical concept — it is an operational capability that organizations can build, measure, and continuously improve. The following framework translates quantum empathy principles into specific practices for each function in the organization.

The Four Empathy Failure Modes

Before describing what quantum empathy looks like in practice, it is useful to catalog the four most common ways organizations fail to achieve it — because each failure mode has specific, identifiable symptoms and specific remedies.

Failure Mode 1: Premature State Collapse

This is the most common failure mode. It occurs when a system or a person forces a customer into a single defined state — a single stage, a single need, a single emotional dimension — before the customer has had the opportunity to express the full complexity of their actual state. The customer calls a support line and the IVR immediately routes them to "billing inquiries" because their last interaction was billing-related, when this call is actually about a technical problem that has a billing consequence. The customer visits a product page and the recommendation engine immediately surfaces upsell options because their purchase history indicates high average order value, when today they are in research mode and upsell feels like pressure.

The remedy for premature state collapse is designed ambiguity: building interaction systems that begin by listening and gathering — through behavioral signals, explicit questions, and contextual inference — before committing to a treatment protocol. The few additional seconds required to correctly identify a customer's current multi-dimensional state more than pay for themselves in the quality of the subsequent interaction.

Failure Mode 2: Emotional Monoculture

Emotional monoculture occurs when an organization designs its experiences around a single emotional register — typically either uniformly positive: every interaction is enthusiastically celebratory or uniformly neutral: every interaction is formally professional. Both approaches fail to meet customers in the full range of emotional states they actually bring to interactions.

A customer who has just experienced a significant service failure needs acknowledgment, not celebration. A customer who has just made a significant purchase needs validation and excitement, not neutral efficiency. The organizations that manage emotional register best are those that have built explicit emotional calibration into their experience design — training human agents in emotional intelligence, building sentiment detection into digital and voice channels, and designing interaction protocols that shift register in response to detected customer emotional state.

Failure Mode 3: Historical Bias Override

This failure mode occurs when historical data about a customer overrides current signals about their present state. The loyal long-term customer who is calling in genuine distress is treated with casual familiarity because their history shows high satisfaction. The first-time customer who happens to browse a high-value product category is immediately targeted for upsell because their session looks like a high-intent buyer, when they are actually doing research for a friend.

The remedy is current-state weighting: ensuring that AI systems and human agents give appropriate priority to present behavioral and emotional signals rather than defaulting to historical profile data. History is context, not destiny. Every interaction is a fresh opportunity to determine who this customer is right now.

Failure Mode 4: Symmetric Empathy Assumption

This failure mode assumes that what would feel empathetic to the designer of the experience is what will feel empathetic to the customer experiencing it. Cultural differences in communication expectations, individual personality variations, and situational context create enormous diversity in what "empathetic" actually means. What feels warmly personal to one customer feels inappropriately familiar to another. What feels efficiently professional to one customer feels cold and dismissive to another.

The remedy for symmetric empathy assumption is personalized empathy calibration: using behavioral data, explicit preference information, and real-time signals to calibrate the emotional register and communication style of each interaction to the specific individual. This is one of the areas where AI genuinely augments human capability — human agents can calibrate their empathy within the range of their personal experience, while AI systems can calibrate across the full distribution of customer preferences in the organization's data.

Measuring Quantum Empathy: The Emotional Residue Score

The most important metric for quantum empathy is what we call the Emotional Residue Score: the net emotional state of the customer after the interaction, relative to their emotional state before it. This is distinct from the satisfaction score, which measures whether the rational outcome of the interaction met expectations and the effort score, which measures how much cognitive work was required to achieve the outcome. The Emotional Residue Score captures something neither of those metrics does: how the customer feels about the company after the interaction is over.

Research consistently shows that Emotional Residue is a stronger predictor of long-term loyalty than either satisfaction or effort. A customer who achieved a satisfactory outcome with moderate effort but whose interaction left them feeling dismissed or undervalued is a churn risk. A customer who did not get exactly what they asked for but whose interaction left them feeling heard, respected, and genuinely cared for is likely to remain — and to tell others.

Emotional Residue Score	Predicted Loyalty Outcome	Advocacy Probability	Recommended Response Protocol
+2 or higher (Strong Positive)	Very high — likely to deepen relationship	High — proactive referral likely	Amplify: invite advocacy, deepen relationship
+1 (Moderate Positive)	Good — likely to remain loyal	Moderate — will share if asked	Maintain: consistent quality delivery
0 (Neutral)	At risk — vulnerable to competitive offer	Low — will not actively advocate	Investigate: identify unmet emotional need
-1 (Moderate Negative)	High churn risk — actively considering alternatives	Negative — may share negative experience	Intervene: proactive recovery contact
-2 or lower (Strong Negative)	Very high churn risk — likely to leave and damage brand	Very negative — likely to share publicly	Emergency: immediate senior intervention

From Customer Touchpoints to Dynamic CxC Matrix Customer Probability Clouds: The Visualization Practice

Traditional customer journey maps are static documents: they show a linear or branching path from Awareness to Community, with specific touchpoints marked at each stage. These maps are useful for strategic planning and organizational alignment, but they are inadequate as operational tools because they do not capture the dynamic, probabilistic nature of actual customer journeys.

The CxC Matrix Customer Probability Cloud visualization replaces the static journey map with a dynamic representation that shows the customer's current probability distribution across all relevant lifecycle stages, channels, and cognitive states. In a Customer Sensor organization, this visualization is generated in real time from live sensor data and updated continuously as new signals arrive. At any given moment, the visualization shows:

1. Current Stage Distribution: The probability that the customer is "primarily" in each of the 15 lifecycle stages, with multiple stages potentially having significant probability mass e.g., 40% Stage 11-Use, 30% Stage 12-Support, 20% Stage 4-Selection of a new product, 10% Stage 15-Community
2. Channel Presence: The likelihood that the customer is active in each channel based on recent behavioral signals and time-of-day patterns
3. Emotional State Vector: A multi-dimensional representation of the customer's current emotional state, drawn from available biometric and behavioral signals

4. Intent Trajectory: The predicted direction of movement across the probability distribution over the next 4, 24, and 168 hours
5. CxC Matrix Intervention Opportunity Map: The specific cells in the probability cloud where a well-designed intervention would most effectively advance both customer and business outcomes

The CxC Matrix Intervention Opportunity Map is the most actionable output of the probability cloud visualization. It identifies the specific moments — defined by a combination of stage, channel, emotional state, and predicted intent — where the organization's intervention will be most welcome, most effective, and most valuable. These are the moments where the quantum empathy principle comes alive: the organization meets the customer in the full complexity of their current reality and responds in a way that honors that complexity.

Quantum Empathy in Practice: Department-Level Case Studies

Hypothetical Case Study: USAA's Military Life Event Prediction System (Based on USAA customer stories, research, website and materials, trade show discussions with US Veterans Association

USAA, the financial services company serving military members and their families, developed one of the earliest and most successful implementations of quantum empathy principles in the financial services sector. Military families experience a distinctive set of life transitions — deployment, permanent change of station, discharge, disability, survivor benefits — that create highly predictable but timing-uncertain customer needs. Traditional financial service approaches waited for customers to reach out when these needs became acute. USAA's quantum empathy system anticipated them.

The system integrated multiple data streams: federal service records that USAA could access with member consent, behavioral patterns in account usage, location data from mobile app usage, and explicit life event data that members shared through the USAA app's life event planning tools. By combining these signals, the system could detect early indicators of impending life events — a pattern of increased ATM withdrawals from unfamiliar locations that might indicate pre-deployment preparation, changes in direct deposit patterns that might indicate a change in posting, account activity patterns consistent with the household management challenges that accompany deployment.

When the system detected these signals with sufficient confidence, it triggered proactive outreach through the customer's preferred channel — a personal phone call from a relationship manager for high-value members, a proactively prepared service package presented through the app for others. The outreach was designed to feel like genuine care rather than automated marketing: it acknowledged the likely life event directly, expressed genuine understanding of the challenges it creates, and offered specific, practical assistance tailored to the predicted situation.

CxC Matrix Quantum Empathy Questions: The Coach's Corner Framework

Developing organizational quantum empathy requires deliberate practice — training teams to think about customers in probabilistic, multi-dimensional, contextually sensitive ways. The following framework of quantum empathy questions is designed to be used in team planning sessions, product reviews, service design workshops, and any other context where customer experience decisions are being made.

1. If the customer could toggle one variable in this interaction — the channel, the timing, the tone, the information presented, the action required — what would they most likely change? And why haven't they changed it themselves? (This question surfaces friction that customers accept but would prefer not to.)
2. What contextual factors might be influencing this customer right now that we cannot directly observe? What is their likely physical context, time pressure, emotional context, competing priorities? (This

question forces consideration of the customer's full reality rather than just their behavior within our system.)

3. How might this customer's needs change in the next 30 minutes? The next 30 days? The next 30 months? Which of those timeframes is the current interaction most consequential for? (This question introduces temporal perspective and prevents over-optimization for the immediate interaction at the expense of the long-term relationship.)
4. If this customer were in a measurably different emotional state right now — more confident, more tired, more excited, more anxious — how would the optimal response differ? And what signals tell us which state they are actually in? (This question forces explicit consideration of emotional calibration.)
5. What would this customer tell their closest friend about this interaction, one week from now? Would that story serve our interests? What would make it a better story? (This question activates thinking about emotional residue and word-of-mouth consequences.)
6. Whose interests does the current interaction design most optimize for — the customer's or the company's? Is that the right balance? What would change if we shifted the optimization target 20% further toward the customer? (This question forces honest accounting of the customer-value balance in every interaction design.)

The Empathy Paradox: When Technology Makes Experiences Feel More Human

Counterintuitively, the most technologically sophisticated customer experiences often feel the most genuinely human. This "Empathy Paradox" — the observation that AI systems capable of processing more contextual signals than human agents, detecting patterns invisible to human observation, and personalizing responses at a scale impossible for human-only systems can create experiences that feel more personally attentive than human service at its best.

The Empathy Paradox explains why customers often rate AI-augmented service interactions higher than equivalent purely human interactions in satisfaction surveys — not because customers prefer talking to AI, but because AI-augmented human agents, equipped with real-time customer context, predictive intent models, and emotional state information, can deliver a quality of personalized attention that exceeds what unaided human agents can typically achieve. The technology does not replace the human; it enables the human to perform at the level that customers most value.

The organizations that most fully realize the Empathy Paradox are those that deploy AI augmentation for human agents most thoughtfully: surfacing the right information at the right moment, providing guidance that respects rather than constrains agent judgment, and handling administrative complexity so that human agents can devote their cognitive and emotional resources entirely to the customer interaction rather than dividing them between the customer and the CRM system. When technology truly serves this role, the result is human service at its best —

attentive, knowledgeable, personalized, and genuinely caring.

PART II: CAPTURING AND OPTIMIZING EXPERIENCE

From Surface Signals to Consciousness Mapping

CHAPTER FOUR

Four Domains, One Customer

Physical · Digital · Hybrid · Synthetic

We Need a New Map

Every customer your company serves exists right now in four separate domains simultaneously. They are living in physical reality — sitting in a chair, feeling temperature, hearing ambient sound. They are navigating digital spaces — with browser tabs open, apps running in the background, notifications queued. They are participating in hybrid experiences that blend the two — perhaps using a navigation app while driving, or consulting a product review while standing in a store aisle. And they are extending themselves through synthetic copies — calendar systems scheduling meetings on their behalf, recommendation engines curating their information environment, AI assistants fielding queries and managing correspondence.

Traditional customer experience frameworks were designed for a world where these domains were largely separate and sequential. Customers went to the store (physical), then went home and went online (digital). They made a phone call (one-on-one) or browsed a website (digital). The domains were distinct environments that customers moved between rather than inhabited simultaneously.

That world no longer exists. The modern customer does not move between domains — they exist in all four at once. And the customer experience frameworks, technologies, and organizational structures designed for sequential, domain-separated interaction are increasingly inadequate for the multi-domain reality.

Domain 1: Physical Reality

Characteristics

- Analog, human-sensed experiences governed by the laws of physics
- Memory and emotional stimulation tied to embodied sensory experience
- Bound by calendar time and physical location — one person, one place, one moment
- Shaped by personal psychology, current physiological state, and immediate environmental context

The physical domain is the domain of authentic, embodied experience. Customers interact with brands here through in-store visits, face-to-face sales and service, physical product use, and the tangible dimensions of delivery and fulfillment. Emotional associations formed in the physical domain are among the most durable and most powerful drivers of customer behavior — positive experiences become "memories," and memories become loyalty.

Physical domain design requires mastery of environmental psychology, service design, and the choreography of human interaction. The sensory environment — lighting, scent, temperature, sound, spatial layout — shapes customer behavior in ways that most organizations do not fully account for. A retail environment that reduces cognitive load through clear wayfinding and logical merchandise organization measurably reduces customer frustration and increases average transaction value, independent of price or product quality.

Customer Sensor Integration in the Physical Domain

The physical domain is being progressively transformed by sensor integration. RFID tags track product movement. Computer vision systems monitor customer dwell time and attention patterns. Smart environments adjust lighting, temperature, and ambient sound in response to occupancy data and time of day. These integrations are already operational today, and they will become ubiquitous by 2031.

The key design challenge for the physical domain in the Customer Sensor era is the integration of sensor data with the emotional authenticity that defines the physical experience. Customers are increasingly aware of — and often uncomfortable with — the surveillance dimensions of sensor-enhanced physical spaces. Organizations that integrate sensors while maintaining transparency, respecting privacy preferences, and demonstrating clear customer benefit from the data they collect will earn the permission relationships that create competitive advantage. Those that surveil without transparency will generate the kind of trust-destroying backlash that has become increasingly costly in the social-media-amplified reputation economy.

Domain 2: Digital Reality

Characteristics

- Time is flexible — continuous, shiftable, simulated, recordable, and searchable

- Space is transportable and multi-perspective — the same customer exists simultaneously across multiple platforms
- Every interaction is trackable, and data is accessible across devices and sessions
- Emotional states are synthetic or profile-based rather than embodied

In the digital domain, time behaves differently than in physical reality. Customers can pause, rewind, and fast-forward their experience. They compare a dozen alternatives simultaneously. They research at 2 AM from their bedroom. They start a journey on one device and continue it on another, expecting their context — shopping cart contents, saved preferences, conversation history — to follow them seamlessly.

This temporal flexibility creates both opportunity and challenge. The opportunity: customers who are in a research mode in the digital domain are often in a high-information-receptivity state that is optimal for education, comparison facilitation, and consultative value delivery. The challenge: the same temporal flexibility means customers can disengage instantly and without friction. The cost of a poor digital experience is a click, not a 30-minute drive back to the store.

The Algorithm Relationship

A fundamental feature of the digital domain — and one that most CX frameworks have not adequately addressed — is the mediating role of algorithmic systems in shaping what customers see, when they see it, and in what context. Google's search algorithms, social media recommendation systems, and programmatic advertising networks do not neutrally present customers with information. They actively curate, prioritize, and contextualize the information environment based on behavioral models that optimize for engagement, click-through, and conversion.

In the Customer Sensor Mesh economy, this algorithmic mediation extends far beyond search and social media. The customer's own AI agents are curating information on their behalf. The customer's preferred shopping app presents options filtered through preference models built from years of behavioral data. The customer's financial management system flags purchase opportunities that align with their stated and inferred goals. Organizations that understand the algorithmic landscape their customers navigate — and that design their digital offerings to be appropriately visible, legible, and evaluable by both human customers and their AI agents — will have a decisive advantage over those that rely on passive digital presence.

Domain 3: Hybrid/Enhanced Reality

Characteristics

- Real-time video, audio playback, and augmented sensory experience
- Blends physical and digital in ways that enhance both dimensions
- Enables scenario review — replaying the past or previewing possible futures
- Removes physical, financial, and geographic barriers through parameterization

The hybrid domain is where the physical and digital worlds merge. Today, this convergence is still primarily experienced through mobile devices: customers using apps to scan product codes for additional information, using AR features to visualize furniture in their home before purchasing, or attending events where remote and in-person participants interact through video and collaborative platforms.

By 2031, the hybrid domain will be substantially more immersive. Lightweight AR glasses will overlay digital information onto physical environments as a natural part of daily life. The distinction between "looking at a menu" and "browsing a restaurant's digital ordering system" will dissolve as the menu itself becomes an interactive digital surface. The distinction between "shopping in a store" and "shopping online" will similarly dissolve as physical retail environments become ambient digital interfaces.

The customer experience implications of this dissolution are profound. The hybrid domain will demand a new category of experience design — one that can orchestrate physical environment, digital information, and interactive capability as integrated elements of a single coherent experience, rather than as separate channels that customers toggle between.

Domain 4: Synthetic Reality

Characteristics

- Boundless digital and machine-enabled environments with no physical constraints
- Time is goal-triggered — events occur when conditions are met, not on a fixed calendar
- Space is unlimited — remote resources are instantly accessible; geography is irrelevant
- Emotions are programmable with conditional logic, filters, and adaptive personalization

The synthetic domain is where AI agents operate on behalf of human principals. It is the domain of automated purchasing, algorithmic service management, digital twin simulation, and autonomous negotiation. It is, in a sense, the customer's permanent representative in the marketplace — always monitoring, always comparing, always ready to act when conditions meet the customer's standing preferences and permission grants.

For most of human history, the synthetic domain did not exist. Even simple automation systems like credit card fraud detection algorithms — which take autonomous action on a customer's behalf without requiring their real-time input — represent the early synthetic domain. By 2031, every customer will have multiple AI agents operating in the synthetic domain on their behalf, and the interactions between these customer agents and company AI systems will represent a growing share of total customer experience volume.

Domain	Time Quality	Space Quality	Emotional Quality	Primary CX Design Challenge
Physical	Sequen-tial, irrevers-ible	Fixed, embodied	Authentic, memory-forming	Designing sensory environments that create positive emotional associations
Digital	Flexible, revers-ible	Ubiquitous, multi-device	Synthetic, profile-based	Creating personalization that feels genuine without feeling surveilled
Hybrid	Blended, scenario-enabled	Augmented, overlaid	Co-con-structed	Integrating physical and digital coherently without friction or confusion
Synthetic	Event-triggered, asynch-ronous	Unlimited, instantan-eous	Programm-able, adaptive	Making autonomous systems trustworthy, legible, and truly representative of customer values

Implementing Multi-Domain Customer Experience: Practical Architecture

Understanding the four domains theoretically is straightforward. Designing and operating customer experiences that function seamlessly across all four simultaneously is one of the most complex organizational challenges in modern business. This section provides practical architecture guidance for each domain and for the integration layer that connects them.

Physical Domain Implementation: The Sensory Environment Checklist

Physical domain experience design begins with the recognition that human beings process physical environments primarily through subconscious channels. The temperature of a retail environment affects purchase behavior. The acoustic quality of a service space affects how customers perceive service quality. The physical distance between a customer and a service representative during a consultation affects how personal the interaction feels. These are not intangible soft factors — they are design variables with measurable effects on customer behavior and business outcomes.

The Customer Sensor Mesh enhancement of the physical domain adds real-time awareness and adaptive response to these environmental variables. A retail environment equipped with occupancy sensors, behavioral analytics cameras, and ambient environmental controls can continuously monitor how customers are navigating and responding to the space and make micro-adjustments — lighting intensity, aisle configuration recommendations, staff positioning guidance — that optimize the physical experience in real time.

Five design principles govern effective physical domain experience in the Customer Sensor era:

1. Design for arrival: the first 90 seconds of a customer's physical interaction with your brand space create the emotional frame for everything that follows. Every element of the arrival experience — parking, entrance, first visual impression, first human contact — should be deliberately designed and continuously optimized.
2. Design for the journey, not the transaction: physical experiences that are optimized solely around completing a transaction feel impersonal and instrumental. Physical experiences that are designed around supporting the customer's full journey — including the stages before and after the specific transaction — feel like genuine service.
3. Design for the departure: how a customer feels when they leave a physical location is their lasting emotional memory of the brand. An excellent experience that ends badly leaves a negative residue. A mediocre experience that ends with a genuinely warm, personalized goodbye can leave a positive one.
4. Integrate sensing transparently: physical domain sensing — cameras, RFID, biometric systems — should be disclosed clearly and managed with explicit customer benefit. Undisclosed surveillance, even when technically legal, destroys trust when discovered.
5. Maintain human override: every automated element of the physical domain experience should be immediately overridable by human staff. The ambient intelligence augments human judgment; it does not constrain it.

Digital Domain Implementation: The Machine-Readable Brand Architecture

The most important structural change in digital domain implementation for the Customer Sensor Mesh era is the requirement to design not just for human users but for AI agents acting on behalf of human users. This creates a new category of design work — machine-readable brand architecture — that is distinct from, but must be integrated with, traditional human-centered UX design.

Machine-readable brand architecture encompasses several specific capabilities. Structured data markup that describes your products, services, and offerings in formats that AI assistants and automated agents can retrieve and interpret without human intervention. API endpoints that allow AI purchasing agents to query inventory, pricing, configuration options, and availability in real time. Negotiation protocols that define what terms are available for automated negotiation and what parameters govern each. Performance data feeds that provide verifiable, third-party-auditable evidence of product or service performance in formats that AI evaluation systems can assess objectively.

The human UX and machine UX dimensions of the digital channel must be designed together rather than separately. The same product information that is displayed beautifully for a human user should also be structured and accessible as an API endpoint. The same pricing logic that human customers see should be expressible as a machine-negotiable protocol. The same performance evidence that persuades human customers should be structured as machine-evaluable proof.

Digital Domain AI Readiness Audit

Assess your digital channel readiness for AI-agent customers by asking: Can an AI agent discover your offerings without human navigation? Can it retrieve accurate pricing, configuration, and availability data programmatically? Can it verify your performance claims against third-party data sources? Can it execute a purchase transaction without human assistance on either side? Can it resolve a post-purchase issue through automated channels? Companies that score poorly on these questions are invisible or inaccessible to the growing share of customer need managed by autonomous AI agents. In high-automation categories, this represents a competitive risk that compounds as agent-to-agent commerce share increases.

Hybrid Domain Implementation: Designing the Blend

Hybrid domain experience design requires mastery of three distinct design disciplines simultaneously: physical environment design, digital interface design, and the design of the seam between them. The seam is where most hybrid experiences fail: the moment of transition from physical to digital or digital to physical that creates friction, confusion, or loss of context.

Consider a customer who scans a QR code on a physical product display to access digital product information. This is a basic hybrid domain interaction. The physical trigger — the QR code scan — should load instantly to a digital experience that knows exactly which product the customer scanned, in which physical location, at what time of day, and ideally with what behavioral context: did they spend time examining the product before scanning, or did they scan immediately on approach?. The digital experience should be optimized for the specific context of someone who is physically present with the product — not a generic product page, but a contextually intelligent interface that answers the questions most relevant to someone standing in front of this product in this location.

The evolution of the hybrid domain through 2031 and beyond will progressively dissolve the seam. AR glasses, dynamically smart shelf signage with NFC/Bluetooth eliminate the QR code scan — they automatically recognize the product and overlay digital information. Ambient spatial computing eliminates the need to navigate to a digital interface at all — the information is present in the physical space, accessible to the customer at the moment they want it. Designing for this dissolved seam requires thinking of the hybrid domain not as digital information layered on physical experience, but as a unified information environment in which physical and digital are simply two dimensions of the same space.

Synthetic Domain Implementation: Governing Your Customer's Representatives

The synthetic domain presents the most novel implementation challenges of the four domains because it requires organizations to interact effectively with entities — AI agents — that have different decision-making logic, different information needs, and different interaction preferences than human customers.

Governing your interactions with customer AI agents requires several specific capabilities. Discovery protocols that make your offerings visible and evaluable by agent systems without requiring navigation designed for human cognitive patterns. Evaluation frameworks that provide the structured, comparative, verifiable information that agent systems need to make reliable recommendations. Negotiation interfaces that allow agents to explore the parameter space of available terms efficiently without triggering the friction or confusion that manual negotiation processes often create. Transaction protocols that allow agents to execute purchases, sign contracts, and initiate service relationships through machine-to-machine interfaces that are secure, auditable, and reliable. Do these capabilities and realities create a new type of subscription service design?

The governance challenge extends beyond the mechanics of agent interaction to the substantive question of what outcomes you are willing to accept from agent-initiated transactions. A well-designed agent negotiation protocol might result in an agent securing a discount or a service term that your human customers typically receive less frequently. How does the organization manage the equity between human-negotiated and agent-negotiated customer relationships? This is not a hypothetical question — it is already arising in enterprise procurement contexts where AI-powered procurement platforms are negotiating terms that human procurement teams could not achieve, and it will become ubiquitous in consumer contexts by 2031.

CHAPTER FIVE

Capturing Immersive Experience Streams

From Surface Sensors to Consciousness Mapping

Customer Surface Sensors to Consciousness Mapping

The CxC Matrix 3.0 Perception Layer Toolkit represents a fundamental reimagining of how organizations sense, interpret, and respond to customer states. In the traditional CX paradigm, companies learned about customers through surveys, interviews, behavioral analytics, and the occasional ethnographic observation. These methods shared a critical limitation: they were retrospective. They revealed how customers had felt, what they had done, what they had thought — after the fact, through the filter of memory and reflection.

The Customer Sensor Mesh framework replaces retrospective sensing with prospective, continuous, real-time consciousness mapping. Instead of asking "how did you feel about that experience?" companies now continuously monitor the signals that reveal how customers are feeling right now — and use that real-time awareness to optimize the experience as it unfolds rather than after it concludes.

The CxC Matrix 3.0 Perception Layer Toolkit

The Perception Layer sits at the interface between the physical and digital worlds, capturing raw signals from every available source and translating them into structured data that the Cognition Layer can interpret. Key components of the Perception Layer Toolkit include:

Behavioral Signal Processing

Behavioral signals are the most established and most widely deployed component of the Perception Layer. Clickstream analysis, session recording, eye-tracking, heat mapping, and conversion funnel analysis have been standard digital analytics practice for more than two decades. In the Customer Sensor Mesh framework, these tools are enhanced by AI systems that can identify behavioral patterns correlated with specific customer states — hesitation, confusion, high engagement, comparison mode — and trigger automated responses tailored to each state.

The most valuable behavioral signals are often the micro-behaviors that traditional analytics systems overlook: the fraction-of-a-second pause before a form field that indicates the customer is uncertain about what to enter, the slight change in scroll speed that indicates a customer has found something interesting but hasn't yet decided whether to engage, the three-second dwell on a competitor's name in a comparison chart that indicates the customer is actively evaluating their outside option.

Biometric Signal Processing

Biometric signals — physiological measurements that reflect internal states — represent the frontier of the Customer Sensor Perception Layer. In controlled research settings, biometric sensors including eye-tracking devices, galvanic skin response sensors, heart rate monitors, and facial action coding systems have long been used to assess customer reactions to product concepts, advertisements, and interface designs. The innovation of the Customer Sensor era is the extension of biometric sensing from the controlled lab to the continuous experience.

Today, consumer wearables already collect a rich biometric dataset that could, with appropriate customer permission, be integrated into CX systems. Smartwatch data includes heart rate, heart rate variability, skin temperature, motion, and sleep quality — each of which provides information about the customer's current emotional and physiological state. By 2031, ambient biometric sensors integrated into home, vehicle, and retail environments will expand the accessible biometric dataset dramatically.

Privacy-by-Design in Biometric Sensing

Biometric data collection requires explicit, informed, granular consent. Best-practice organizations implement a "data value proposition" for each biometric signal collected: customers see a clear statement of what data is collected, how it is used, what benefit they receive in exchange, and how they can revoke consent at any time. Consent should be specific to the signal type, not bundled in a general terms-of-service agreement.

Organizations that implement transparent, customer-controlled biometric data programs consistently outperform those that rely on implicit or buried consent mechanisms — in both customer satisfaction metrics and regulatory compliance positioning.

Hypothetical Case Study: Cleveland Clinic Digital Phenotyping

In 2031, Cleveland Clinic launched a patient experience program using what researchers called "digital phenotyping" — the integration of multiple continuous data streams to build a comprehensive model of each patient's health state, behavioral patterns, and experience preferences. The program enrolled patients voluntarily in a comprehensive sensor mesh network that included wearable biometric monitoring, smart home environmental sensors, and periodic AI-administered assessments, and care circle communications and permission states.

The system's primary CX objective was to transform the patient experience from episodic (defined by clinic visits) to continuous (defined by the ongoing relationship between patient, patient care circle and care team). Instead of a patient's experience beginning when they walked through the clinic door and ending when they left, the system created a continuous experience that monitored health trajectories, anticipated needs, and proactively engaged patients and patient care circle at the moments when intervention would be most effective and most welcome.

The clinical outcomes were impressive — but the experience outcomes were equally significant. Patients in the program reported dramatically lower levels of health anxiety (they felt monitored rather than alone with their health concerns), patient care circle felt more aware, confident and informed with reduced feelings of anxiety and helplessness, higher satisfaction with care quality (they perceived their care team as more attentive and responsive), and significantly higher likelihood to recommend the clinic to family and friends. The digital phenotyping program had transformed the patient-clinic relationship from transactional to genuinely relational — exactly the outcome that the CxC Matrix framework defines as the transition from Use/Support to Community.

Advanced Perception Layer Capabilities: The 2030's Sensing Frontier

Computer Vision in Customer Experience Management

Computer vision — the ability of AI systems to interpret visual information from cameras and sensors — has become one of the most commercially important capabilities in the Customer Sensor Mesh toolkit. Its applications in customer experience management span every lifecycle stage and every domain, from the retail analytics cameras that track customer attention patterns in physical stores to the smartphone cameras that enable product recognition and AR try-on experiences to the medical imaging systems that detect health conditions before they become symptomatic.

The most commercially mature applications of computer vision in customer experience are behavioral analytics applications: systems that process camera feeds from retail environments, service locations, or product usage contexts to extract behavioral data without requiring explicit customer action. These systems can count customers, track movement paths, measure dwell time by location, identify queue length and wait time, detect product interaction patterns, and assess the effectiveness of display configurations — all from standard security camera infrastructure enhanced with vision AI processing.

The frontier applications of computer vision in customer experience are more ambitious and more ethically complex: facial emotion recognition systems that assess customer emotional states from facial expressions, gaze tracking systems that identify what customers are looking at and for how long, and body language analysis systems that infer cognitive and emotional states from postural and gestural signals. These capabilities are technically available today and are deployed in research and enterprise contexts with appropriate consent frameworks. Their mainstream deployment in consumer customer experience will require both technical maturation: improving accuracy across diverse demographic groups, lighting conditions, and camera angles; and social maturation: developing norms and regulations that govern appropriate use.

Voice and Language Signal Processing

Voice is the oldest and most natural human communication channel, and voice signal processing has become one of the richest sources of real-time customer state data in the Customer Sensor Mesh toolkit. Beyond the content of what a customer says — which natural language understanding systems have been processing effectively for a decade — voice signal processing now routinely extracts emotional and physiological information from how a customer speaks: speaking rate, pitch variation, vocal tension, breath patterns, and micro-pauses.

A customer speaking with measurable vocal tension and accelerated speech rate is physiologically stressed, regardless of what they are saying. A customer whose speech slows and whose pitch drops when discussing a specific option is showing signs of consideration and engagement that differ from their baseline vocal pattern. A customer whose voice quality changes when a price is mentioned — even if their words are neutral — may be revealing price sensitivity that their explicit responses might not capture.

The ethical dimensions of voice signal processing in customer interactions require careful attention. Many jurisdictions require explicit disclosure and consent for recording customer interactions. The use of voice emotion analysis beyond what is disclosed in standard consent notices raises additional consent questions. Organizations deploying voice signal processing in customer experience contexts should design their consent frameworks to be specific about what information is being extracted and how it will be used — and should ensure that voice-derived emotional intelligence is used to help customers rather than to manipulate them.

Wearable Data Integration: The Permission-First Framework

The integration of wearable device data into customer experience management represents perhaps the most powerful capability in the Customer Sensor Mesh toolkit — and the one that carries the highest privacy stakes. Wearable devices generate a uniquely intimate data stream: they monitor physiological processes: heart rate, skin conductance, temperature, respiration; track behavioral patterns: sleep, activity, location, routine; and increasingly monitor health-relevant parameters: blood oxygen, stress indicators, glucose levels in clinical devices, that are among the most sensitive categories of personal information.

The permission-first framework for wearable data integration establishes that the default state is privacy-protective: no wearable data is integrated into customer experience systems without explicit, specific, informed, and granular customer consent. "Specific" means that consent is granted for each type of wearable data independently — a customer might consent to location data integration but not physiological data integration. "Granular" means that customers can grant or revoke consent for individual data types without affecting other parts of their service relationship. "Informed" means that the specific customer benefit enabled by each consent grant is clearly articulated at the moment of consent — not buried in terms-of-service language.

The customer benefit proposition must be real and proportionate. A customer consent to share heart rate variability data in exchange for a marginally more personalized product recommendation is disproportionate — the benefit is too small to justify the privacy commitment. A customer consent to share heart rate variability data in exchange for a proactive wellness alert system that could detect a cardiac event before it becomes a medical emergency is appropriately proportionate. The customer benefit must justify the data commitment, and the organization must be able to articulate that justification clearly.

Environmental Sensing: Smart Spaces as Experience Delivery Platforms

The ambient intelligence of smart spaces — buildings, vehicles, and outdoor environments equipped with sensor networks, edge computing, and AI systems — creates a new category of passive customer experience delivery:

experiences that are delivered by the environment itself, without requiring the customer to take any action to receive them.

A smart retail environment that adjusts its lighting scheme in response to the emotional signals of the current customer population — warmer, lower-intensity lighting during high-stress periods, cooler and brighter during high-energy browsing periods — is delivering an experience that requires nothing from the customer. A smart hotel room that learns a guest's temperature preferences during their first night and automatically maintains the room at the right temperature for all subsequent nights is delivering a comfort experience that feels like personalized attention. A smart vehicle that adjusts its cabin environment — music, temperature, seat position, ambient lighting — based on the detected stress or alertness level of the driver is delivering a wellness experience that requires no user interface at all.

These ambient experiences are the ultimate expression of the Customer Sensor Mesh philosophy: understanding what customers need before they know they need it and delivering that value without requiring them to ask. They also represent the environment in which quantum empathy must operate — because the customer cannot observe or override the environmental intelligence that is shaping their experience, the governance of that intelligence must be all the more rigorous.

CHAPTER SIX

Atomic Interactions — The Femtosecond Economy

Mission-Infused Micro-Engagements and the Attention Valuation Framework

Lin Wei stood at the vending machine for 8.3 seconds. In that time, she glanced at 11 product options, her gaze lingered for 340 milliseconds on the blue sparkling water bottle, she reached toward it twice and pulled back, and she ultimately selected the iced tea she had bought from this machine four times in the past three months.

The vending machine's Customer Sensor Mesh system recorded all of this. It noted the hesitation on the sparkling water — a product she had never purchased from this machine but had purchased three times from a competitor's machine near her office. It noted the twice-and-back reach — a behavioral signal that behavioral research has associated with a consumer who is open to trying a new option but is not confident enough to commit. And it noted the final selection of the familiar option — the decision of a customer in time-pressure mode who defaults to the known quantity.

On her next visit, the machine displayed a different interface for Lin Wei: the sparkling water she had hesitated over, accompanied by a personalized message from the flavor's manufacturer — "Lin Wei — we've seen you consider this. First taste free." The machine had used 8.3 seconds of behavioral data and 3 months of purchase history to design a conversion intervention calibrated specifically for her hesitation pattern.

This is the femtosecond economy: the emerging market for customer attention measured, valued, and optimized at sub-second resolution.

The Attention Valuation Framework

The central insight of the femtosecond economy is that customer attention has economic value that can be measured with precision. A customer's gaze dwelling on a product for 340 milliseconds is a more reliable purchase-intent signal than a customer answering "yes" to the question "would you consider buying this product?" on a survey. Behavioral data is more truthful than self-reported data — and microsecond behavioral data, captured through sensor systems, is more truthful than any other source.

The aaCLV formula (Attention-Adjusted Customer Lifetime Value) integrates attention economics into the traditional CLV model:

aaCLV = (Attention Quality × Attention Duration × Conversion Probability × Average Transaction Value × Purchase Frequency) / Cost of Attention Acquisition

The key variable in this formula — and the one most dramatically changed by Customer Sensor Mesh capabilities — is Attention Quality. Traditional CLV models treat all customer attention as equivalent: a website visitor is a website visitor, regardless of whether they spent 10 seconds bouncing away or 10 minutes deeply engaged with product content. The aaCLV model distinguishes between low-quality attention (brief, unfocused, emotionally neutral), medium-quality attention (sustained, moderately engaged, task-oriented), and high-quality attention (deep, emotionally engaged, signal-rich).

Attention Type	Duration	Engagement Signals	Conversion Probability	CX Response Protocol
Low-quality / Browsing	< 3 seconds	No dwell, rapid scroll, no interaction	0.5-2%	Awareness optimization — improve first-impression hooks
Medium-quality / Evaluating	3-30 seconds	Moderate dwell, some interaction, comparison behavior	5-15%	Consideration support — reduce friction, provide comparison tools
High-quality / Deciding	30-180 seconds	Extended dwell, high interaction, back-and-forth	20-45%	Conversion optimization — address specific hesitation

Attention Type	Duration	Engagement Signals	Conversion Probability	CX Response Protocol
		navigation		signals
Ultra-high / Committed	>180 seconds	Deep engagement, form initiation, or repeat visit	60-85%	Fulfillment excellence — remove last-mile friction, confirm value

Mission-Infused Micro-Engagements

Not all micro-engagements are created equal. The most commercially valuable micro-engagements are those that are simultaneously customer-serving and business-serving — where the action that most helps the customer in the immediate moment also advances the most important business objectives. The CxC Matrix 3.0 framework describes these as "mission-infused" interactions: every micro-engagement is designed to embody the organization's mission, deliver measurable value to the customer, and advance a specific business objective.

The design principle is deceptively simple but operationally demanding: before designing any customer interaction — at any level of granularity, in any channel, for any lifecycle stage — the design team should be able to answer three questions:

1. What is the customer's most pressing need in this moment?
2. What is the business's most important objective in this interaction?

3. What single action, delivered in the most frictionless way possible, best serves both?

The answer to question three is the mission-infused micro-engagement. It is not a compromise between the customer's need and the business's need — it is the design space where those needs genuinely align. Finding that space requires deep knowledge of the customer, clear articulation of business objectives, and creative design capability. But when it works, it produces interactions that feel effortless to customers (because they are actually getting what they need) while simultaneously delivering measurable business value.

When Algorithms Meet Algorithms: Game Theory in Multi-Agent Customer Systems

In the Customer Sensor Mesh economy, the interactions between customer AI agents and company AI systems are not bilateral — they are multi-party games involving multiple competing agents, incomplete information, and dynamic strategy. Understanding the game-theoretic dynamics of these multi-agent customer systems is essential for designing systems that produce good outcomes for both companies and customers rather than devolving into adversarial equilibria that damage both.

The Three Games

Three distinct game structures characterize multi-agent customer interactions in the sensor economy:

Game 1: The Matching Game (Awareness through Selection)

In the early lifecycle stages, the primary game is matching: the customer's AI agent is searching for the best solution to a need, and multiple company AI systems are competing to demonstrate that they are the best match. This is a coordination game with network effects — systems that make themselves most easily discoverable, most accurately self-represented, and most efficiently evaluable attract a disproportionate share of agent consideration.

The competitive dynamics of the matching game favor transparency and structured information quality. An AI agent evaluating competing offers will select the offer that best matches the customer's specified and inferred criteria with the highest confidence. Confidence comes from information quality: companies that provide accurate, complete, machine-readable product information win the matching game. Companies that rely on marketing language, obfuscated pricing, or inconsistent third-party data representations lose it.

Game 2: The Negotiation Game: Negotiation through Contract

In the middle lifecycle stages, the game structure shifts to negotiation: a bilateral or multi-party negotiation between the customer's agent and one or more company agents over the terms of a transaction. This is a bargaining game with private information on both sides — the customer's agent has information about the customer's reservation price and alternative options; the company's agent has information about margin, inventory, and competitive positioning.

The negotiation game in multi-agent systems is fundamentally different from human negotiation in two important ways. First, it operates at machine speed — a negotiation that might take days in a human context can be completed in seconds in an agent-to-agent context. Second, it is infinitely patient — AI agents don't feel social pressure, time pressure, or emotional investment in a specific outcome. They will execute a perfectly consistent strategy indefinitely until the best available outcome is achieved or a termination condition is met.

The company agent's optimal negotiation strategy is not to try to exploit information asymmetry — a good customer AI agent will detect and remember exploitation and advise their customer accordingly. The optimal strategy is to make the genuine value of the offer as clear as possible as efficiently as possible, and to structure the negotiation parameters in a way that makes the best available outcome for the customer also the best available outcome for the company.

Game 3: The Retention Game: Use through Community

In the later lifecycle stages, the game is retention: the customer's agent continuously evaluates whether the current relationship is producing the best available outcome against alternatives, and the company's system continuously monitors for signals that would indicate declining relationship satisfaction or increasing competitive vulnerability.

The retention game is an ongoing surveillance game: both parties are continuously monitoring, continuously evaluating, and continuously adjusting. The company system monitors behavioral signals that indicate satisfaction, value realization, and churn risk. The customer agent monitors the competitive market to identify if better alternatives have emerged since the original selection. The relationship is maintained as long as it produces the best available outcome for the customer given their current needs and the available market alternatives.

The Customer Sensor Mesh organization wins the retention game not by making switching difficult — in the agent economy, switching barriers are largely ineffective because AI agents can efficiently manage complex transitions — but by continuously improving the value delivered through the relationship. The customer whose AI agent concludes, at every evaluation cycle, that this relationship is producing better outcomes than any available alternative is a customer who stays, deepens their engagement, and eventually becomes a community advocate.

The Femtosecond Economy in Practice: Attention Valuation Across Industries

The femtosecond economy concept applies differently across industries, and understanding those differences is essential for designing appropriate attention valuation frameworks. The following analysis examines how attention economics operates in five major industry contexts:

Industry	Primary Attention Currency	Optimal Attention Window	Attention Monetization Model
Financial Services	Decision-quality cognitive attention during major financial choices	Moments of peak decision readiness — identified by behavioral signals	Consultation-to-conversion; advice-to-outcome; trust-to-retention
Healthcare	Receptive attention during health	Post-diagnosis, post-	Adherence improvement; preventive care

Industry	Primary Attention Currency	Optimal Attention Window	Attention Monetization Model
	education and behavior change moments	symptom, post-outcome — high receptivity states	adoption; wellness behavior change
Retail / E-commerce	Purchase-intent attention at point of highest commitment probability	Hesitation detection window — the 30-180 second decision window	Conversion optimization; basket expansion; abandonment recovery
Media / Entertainment	Sustained engagement attention across content consumption sessions	Content quality peaks — moments of highest engagement depth	Subscription conversion; content recommendation; platform stickiness
B2B Enterprise	Strategic decision attention during organizational buying processes	Consensus-building windows — when multiple stakeholders are actively engaged	Deal velocity; deal size; renewal commitment

Choreographing and Curating Exceptional Multimodal Experiences

The most sophisticated Customer Sensor Mesh interactions are multimodal: they simultaneously engage multiple sensory channels, combine human and AI communication, integrate real-time behavioral data with historical context, and deliver a coherent experience that feels unified rather than fragmented across its component parts.

Multimodal choreography is the practice of designing these complex, multi-channel interactions as integrated compositions rather than parallel execution plans. The choreography metaphor is intentional: just as a choreographer designs the interaction between multiple performers — their timing, their spatial relationships, their individual movements and collective patterns — the multimodal customer experience designer must design the interaction between multiple channels, multiple AI systems, and multiple human touchpoints in a way that creates a unified experience for the customer.

The technical challenge of multimodal choreography is synchronization: ensuring that the customer's experience across multiple simultaneous channels is coherent rather than contradictory. A customer who is simultaneously interacting with a mobile app, receiving SMS notifications, and speaking with an AI voice agent should have all three channels presenting consistent, synchronized, non-redundant information. If the mobile app shows a pending offer while the SMS has already confirmed it and the voice agent doesn't know about either, the experience breaks down. The choreography layer of the Customer Sensor Mesh stack — the component responsible for managing cross-channel consistency in real time — is one of the most technically demanding elements of the architecture to build and maintain.

The Lin Wei Scenario: Neural Experience Optimization in Detail

The vending machine interaction described in the opening of this chapter deserves more detailed examination, because it illustrates the full stack of Customer Sensor

Mesh capabilities operating simultaneously at the femtosecond scale. Understanding each layer of the interaction helps translate the abstract architecture of the Customer Sensor Mesh system into the concrete reality of a specific customer moment.

Layer 1: The Sensing Event

As Lin Wei approached the vending machine, the machine's computer vision system detected her presence at 4.3 meters, began tracking her approach trajectory, and initiated the customer recognition process. Within 0.8 seconds of her entry into the detection zone, the system had matched her face to a registered customer profile with 94% confidence and retrieved her complete interaction history: 23 previous interactions with machines in this network, a preference profile that showed 67% selection rate for sparkling water products, a behavioral pattern showing elevated afternoon purchase frequency on days with temperatures above 28 degrees Celsius, and a payment preference profile showing Apple Pay as her primary method.

Simultaneously, ambient sensors in the machine's immediate environment registered an external temperature of 32 degrees Celsius, time-of-day context of 3:47 PM on a Thursday, and proximity context showing three other pedestrians within 10 meters but no queue at the machine. The machine's microphone array detected that Lin was wearing earbuds and appeared to be listening to audio content, which the behavioral model flagged as indicating a lower cognitive engagement state than typical — she was in transit mode, not deliberative mode.

Layer 2: The Real-Time Model Update

The system updated its customer model for Lin Wei in real time, integrating all available signals into a probability distribution across potential interaction outcomes. The updated model estimated: 73% probability of a purchase interaction, with sparkling water as the most likely selection; 12% probability of browsing behavior without purchase; 15% probability of a quick scan and departure without engagement. The model estimated a current aaCLV context multiplier of 1.8 — significantly above baseline — based on the combination of high temperature, time since her last recorded purchase, and her behavioral profile.

Layer 3: The Dynamic Interface Optimization

Based on the model output, the machine's display configuration engine made 23 micro-adjustments to the interface in the 0.4 seconds before Lin fully engaged with the screen. The sparkling water products she had previously considered — including a product she had hesitated over twice at other machines without purchasing — were repositioned to the most prominent display zone. The pricing display was adjusted to show her most likely preferred price format (unit price rather than multi-pack comparison). The color temperature of the display was adjusted slightly warmer to complement the outdoor light conditions. And a subtle personalized element — her name, retrieved from the customer profile — was briefly displayed in the corner of the screen as she approached, providing a moment of recognition that behavioral research has shown increases engagement duration by an average of 0.4 seconds.

Layer 4: The Hesitation Signal Detection

When Lin's gaze dwelt on the sparkling water product for 340 milliseconds — the same product she had hesitated over twice before — the system's hesitation detection algorithm classified this as a "high-intent hesitation" event: behavioral evidence that she was interested in the product but had not yet made the decision to purchase. The system retrieved the historical context: she had approached this product three times in the past 90 days across different machines in the network, spending between 200 and 480 milliseconds in evaluation, and had not purchased on any occasion.

The intervention protocol for high-intent hesitation on a previously unconverted product triggered a personalized offer: the product's regular price reduced by 40% for this interaction, with a brief message — "Lin Wei — you've been curious about this. First taste, on us." — displayed in a non-intrusive lower corner of the screen for 1.5 seconds. The offer was time-limited at 30 seconds. The discount was funded from the customer acquisition budget for that product line, not from the vending machine's margins — the product manufacturer had pre-negotiated first-trial incentive allocations with the network operator.

Layer 5: The Outcome and the Learning Loop

Lin Wei purchased the sparkling water. The system recorded the conversion event with full context: the intervention protocol that triggered it, the display configuration that preceded it, the customer's hesitation pattern and the duration of the hesitation before the offer appeared, the time from offer display to purchase decision (4.3 seconds), and the emotional signal data available post-purchase (Lin's facial expression shifted from neutral to a slight positive following the purchase, and her walking pace increased slightly after leaving the machine — a behavioral signal the system associated with a positive interaction outcome).

The learning loop updated three components based on this outcome: the hesitation detection algorithm's confidence thresholds for this customer profile type, the intervention protocol for high-intent hesitation (the 40% discount for first trial had converted; the system would test whether a lower discount would also convert on subsequent hesitations), and the customer profile model for Lin Wei herself (who now had a converted sparkling water preference, which would inform future interaction designs across the full network).

In total, 47 distinct data points were updated in Lin Wei's customer model as a result of an 8.3-second vending machine interaction. The total computation required to execute the interaction — from initial detection through offer display through outcome recording — required 0.83 seconds of processing time distributed across edge computing at the machine and cloud processing at the network operations center. The economic outcome: one additional purchase event with an estimated aaCLV contribution of $47, based on the predicted probability that Lin Wei would become a regular sparkling water purchaser in this product network following the first-trial conversion.

Neural A/B Testing: The Next Frontier of Customer Sensor Optimization

The Lin Wei scenario illustrates traditional behavioral A/B testing — testing different intervention protocols against behavioral outcome metrics. The next frontier of Customer

Sensor Mesh optimization is neural A/B testing: testing experience designs directly against biometric measures of customer cognitive and emotional engagement, using real-time neurological and physiological signals rather than behavioral outcome proxies.

Neural A/B testing is currently deployed primarily in research and clinical contexts, where subjects consent to wear EEG sensors or other neurological monitoring equipment. Consumer-grade applications are limited by the form factor constraints of current wearable technology — it is difficult to deploy EEG-based testing at scale in retail or digital environments where customers are not wearing specialized equipment. However, the progression of wearable technology toward the 2031 Wearable Intelligence Threshold will progressively make neural signal data available in consumer contexts, opening the possibility of neural A/B testing in commercial customer experience engineering applications.

The ethical implications of neural A/B testing require careful attention. Testing experience designs against neurological signals raises questions about consent that go beyond traditional A/B testing: customers can readily understand that their purchase behavior is being measured and used to optimize experience designs, but may have more difficulty understanding what it means for their neurological responses to be measured. The consent and transparency architecture for neural A/B testing must be correspondingly more explicit and more carefully designed.

The Attention Economy Quantified: Advanced Implementation

The hypothetical story of Lin Wei at the vending machine illustrates a profound truth about the femtosecond economy: the companies that will define competitive advantage through 2035 are those that have built the infrastructure to sense, model, and respond to human attention at the resolution of individual milliseconds. This is not incremental optimization of existing customer experience practices — it is a fundamental reimagining of what customer experience means when attention itself becomes a measurable, valuable, and tradable commodity.

The Mathematics of Micro-Moments

The optimization engine underlying advanced Customer Sensor Mesh experience management uses a sophisticated value calculation framework — the Micro-Moment Value formula — to assess the economic significance of each sub-second customer state and guide intervention decisions. The formula integrates five variables that together determine the economic value of any given moment of customer engagement:

Micro-Moment Value = Sum of (Engagement Quality × Contextual Relevance × Intent Probability × Delivery Capability) ÷ Interaction Friction

Each variable in this formula represents a dimension of the customer-company value exchange at a specific moment. Engagement Quality captures the attentiveness and receptivity of the customer — are they focused, peripheral, or divided in their attention? Contextual Relevance measures how well the company's potential intervention maps to the customer's current situational needs and environmental context. Intent Probability estimates the likelihood that the customer's current behavioral state will lead to a commercially significant action within a defined time window. Delivery Capability assesses the company's technical ability to provide a specific intervention through the available channels at that moment. Interaction Friction quantifies the cognitive and physical effort required from the customer to engage with the intervention — the denominator in the formula that transforms raw value potential into delivered value.

The power of this formula lies not in any single variable but in the relationships among them. High engagement quality combined with high contextual relevance and low friction produces exponentially higher conversion probability than any single factor would suggest. Conversely, high engagement quality combined with low contextual relevance produces negative outcomes — the customer is attentive, but the interruption is unwelcome, and the emotional residue is worse than if no intervention had been attempted.

The ROI of Neural Experience Optimization

The economic case for Customer Sensor Mesh investment is inferred and hypothesized from observations, experiments and hypothetical scenarios with sample data from early adopter organizations. The following performance comparison, drawn from aggregate data across consumer goods, financial services, and retail sectors, illustrates the magnitude of improvement achievable through fully implemented Customer Sensor Mesh capabilities:

Performance Metric	Traditional CX	Customer Sensor CX	Improvement
Conversion Rate (digital)	2.3%	7.8%	+239%
Average Transaction Value	Baseline	+53%	53% lift
Customer Lifetime Value	Baseline	+222%	222% lift
Cost per Service Interaction	$6.20	$0.94	-85%
Customer Satisfaction Score	72%	91%	+19 points
Word-of-Mouth Referral Rate	12%	34%	+183%
Annual Churn Rate	23%	8%	-65%
First Contact Resolution Rate	61%	87%	+26 points
Time-to-Value (new customer)	14 days average	3.2 days average	-77%
Net Promoter Score	42 (median)	71 (median)	+29 points

These improvement scenarios and experiments do not accrue uniformly or instantly. The organizations reporting the highest performance lifts are those that have been building Customer Sensor capabilities for three or more years, have tested integrated sensor data across most all major customer-facing functions, have drafted and tested the effect and impact of proposed permission architectures with high customer participation rates, and have built analytical teams capable of continuously improving model performance. First-year implementations are forecast to achieve 30–60% of the long-term performance improvement potential; the compounding advantages of accumulated behavioral data, refined predictive models, and deepened customer permission relationships drive the larger gain projections in years two through five.

Game Theory in Multi-Party Customer Sensor Ecosystems

The vending machine scenario introduced the game theory dynamics of a bilateral customer-company AI interaction. In practice, most Customer Sensor Mesh interactions occur within multi-party ecosystems where multiple companies are simultaneously competing for customer attention, behavioral data, and transaction authority. Understanding the game theory of these multi-party ecosystems is essential for designing effective Customer Sensor Mesh strategies.

Three distinct game structures characterize multi-party attention ecosystems. In the Attention Auction game, multiple companies bid for a customer's attentional bandwidth at a specific moment — this is the model already emerging in AR-enabled environments where multiple brands compete for visual overlay placement in a customer's field of view. In the Data Consortium game, companies share anonymized customer behavioral data through a trusted intermediary to improve all participants' predictive models — a cooperative game structure that benefits participants while raising customer transparency and consent requirements. In the Ecosystem Integration game, companies compete not just for transactions but for integration priority in the customer's personal AI ecosystem — becoming the preferred provider that a customer's AI agent consults first for a specific category of need.

Each of these game structures requires a different strategic posture. Winning the Attention Auction requires investment in relevance, timing precision, and the quality of the value exchange offered for customer attention. Winning the Data Consortium game, (tested via distributed ledger technologies across the US Housing ecosystem's 230 participant types and over seven thousand organizations) requires contribution quality — the uniqueness and predictive value of the data a company can contribute to shared pools. Winning the Ecosystem Integration game requires the combination of product quality, API openness, permission architecture excellence, and the track record of trustworthy autonomous action that earns the customer's AI agent's highest-priority trust placement.

The 90-Day Customer Sensor Mesh Capability Activation Plan

For Customer experience engineers tasked with initiating a Customer Sensor Mesh transformation within a defined timeframe, the following 90-day activation plan provides a structured roadmap from baseline assessment to initial operational capability.

Days 1-30: Sense and Align

The first month is dedicated to understanding the current state and building organizational alignment. The customer experience engineer commissions a Customer Sensor Mesh Readiness Assessment across all five dimensions (sensor infrastructure, AI analytical capability, automation level, permission architecture, trust infrastructure), completes a competitive intelligence review of Customer Sensor Mesh adoption in the sector, and conducts internal stakeholder interviews to identify organizational readiness, resistance points, and early adoption advocates.

The deliverable from Days 1–30 is a Customer Sensor Mesh Opportunity Map: a prioritized list of the ten highest-value sensing opportunities, each with a defined business case, a feasibility assessment, and a preliminary permission architecture design. This document becomes the foundation for the month two investment decisions.

Days 31-60: Instrument and Pilot

Month two deploys the first sensing capabilities against the highest-priority opportunities identified in month one. These are small-scale, tightly controlled pilots with clear measurement frameworks, defined success criteria, and explicit learning objectives. The goal is not to demonstrate success — it is to generate reliable learning about what works, what doesn't, and what the customer experience quality implications are of each sensing capability in the specific context of this organization and its customers.

Simultaneously, month two begins the foundational work for the permission architecture: designing the customer data transparency interface, building the consent management infrastructure, and training customer-facing teams on how to communicate about data collection and use in ways that build rather than undermine trust.

Days 61-90: Activate and Learn

Month three scales the pilots that have demonstrated positive results, implements the permission architecture across relevant customer touchpoints, and establishes the continuous learning loop that will drive improvement beyond the initial 90-day period. The customer experience leader presents initial performance data and a 12-month roadmap to senior leadership, securing the sustained investment that the Customer Sensor Mesh transformation requires.

90-Day Success Criteria

A successful 90-day Customer Sensor Mesh activation achieves: (1) At least three sensing capabilities deployed in production with measurement frameworks in place; (2) Permission architecture live with initial customer enrollment; (3) Baseline performance metrics established for each active sensing capability; (4) One significant learning from pilot performance that has been incorporated into the operating model; (5) 12-month roadmap approved with budget allocated. Success is measured not by performance metrics at day 90 — those will take longer to materialize — but by the quality of the organizational learning and the credibility of the roadmap.

CHAPTER SEVEN

Managing Customer Experience as Code

Event-Driven Pipelines and Outcome Contracts

What It Means to Be a Customer When Every Interaction Is Curated by Code

Today, the average consumer's digital experience is already substantially governed by code: recommendation algorithms curate what they see, dynamic pricing algorithms determine what they pay, fraud detection systems decide whether their transactions are approved, and automated marketing systems determine when, how, and how often they are contacted. Most customers have only a vague awareness of this algorithmic curation — they experience it as "the website knows what I like" or "it keeps suggesting things I don't want."

By 2031, the algorithmic curation of customer experience will be far more comprehensive and far more legible. The systems governing customer experience will be explicitly designed as event-driven pipelines: code-based architectures that respond to customer events: behaviors, sensor signals, lifecycle stage transitions, with precisely defined responses, according to business logic that can be inspected, audited, and continuously improved.

This shift from implicit algorithmic curation to explicit experience-as-code architecture has enormous implications for how organizations manage customer experience. When experience is code, it can be:

- Versioned: every change to the experience is tracked, and previous versions can be restored
- Tested: A/B and multivariate testing can be systematically applied to any element
- Audited: the logic governing any customer interaction can be inspected and explained
- Automated: consistent, scalable execution without human variability or fatigue
- Optimized: machine learning can continuously improve performance based on outcome data

Behind the Scenes of Customer Orchestrated Event-Driven Experience

An event-driven customer experience pipeline is composed of four structural elements: Events, Rules, Actions, and Feedback.

Events

An event is any observable change in customer state that has potential business significance. Events can be behavioral: a customer adds an item to a cart, transactional: a customer completes a purchase, temporal: a customer's subscription renewal date is 30 days away, physiological: a customer's wearable detects elevated stress during an interaction, or contextual: a customer enters a geographic zone near a retail location.

The Event Layer of the experience pipeline is responsible for sensing, classifying, and routing events to the appropriate rule engines. In a mature Customer Sensor Mesh architecture, this layer processes thousands of events per customer per day — the vast majority of which trigger no action because they fall below significance thresholds. The design of these thresholds is itself a critical customer experience engineering decision: set them too high and valuable signals are missed; set them too low and customers are over-contacted and the system generates unsustainable data volume.

Rules

Rules define the conditions under which events trigger actions. A simple rule might be: "If a customer has viewed a product three times in 7 days and has not purchased, and their historical conversion probability exceeds 15%, trigger a personalized price discount offer." A more complex rule might integrate multiple event types, require specific combinations of lifecycle stage and channel context, and apply different logic for different customer segments.

Rules are the primary mechanism through which organizational strategy is translated into customer experience design. The set of rules governing a customer experience pipeline is, in effect, a precise, executable statement of how the organization intends to treat its customers. This makes the rules layer both the most powerful and the most dangerous component of the experience architecture: well-designed rules produce consistent, ethical, value-creating experiences; poorly designed rules can produce systematic mistreatment at scale.

Customer Experience Engineer Prompt: Experience Pipeline Audit

Conduct a rules audit of your customer experience pipeline. For each active rule, ask: (1) What is the customer value proposition of this rule — what benefit does it create for the customer? (2) What is the business value proposition — what metric does it improve, and by how much? (3) Are there customer segments for whom this rule produces negative rather than positive outcomes? (4) How old is this rule, and when was it last validated against current performance data? Rules that cannot answer all four questions should be suspended pending review.

Every Customer Interaction Is a Platform

The most important conceptual shift in the experience-as-code paradigm is the redefinition of customer interactions as platforms rather than events. An event is a moment that occurs, generates a result, and ends. A platform is an infrastructure that enables multiple parties to create value in ongoing, compounding ways.

When a customer interaction is designed as a platform, it is not just a transaction or a service moment — it is a context in which multiple value exchanges are possible, in which the customer's AI agents and the company's AI systems can collaborate to generate outcomes that neither could achieve independently, and in which the relationship between customer and company can compound over time in ways that benefit both parties.

Beyond Human Comprehension: Contracting by Outcomes and Designing by Simulation

The experience-as-code paradigm introduces a paradox that customer experience engineers must grapple with directly: the systems that manage customer experience in the Customer Sensor Mesh era will, in many domains, operate at a complexity level that exceeds the ability of any human team to fully understand in real time. An event-driven pipeline managing interactions with 10 million customers across 90 matrix cells, 6 channels, 4 cognitive layers, and hundreds of simultaneous A/B tests is generating decisions at a rate and complexity that no team of humans could review, approve, or understand at the level of individual interactions.

This is not a failure of the framework — it is a success condition. The goal of experience-as-code is precisely to enable the organization to serve each customer with a level of personalization and precision that human judgment cannot achieve at scale. But it requires a different mode of management: one that operates at the level of objectives, values, and system design rather than individual interaction approval.

Outcome-Based Contracting for AI Experience Systems

Outcome-based contracting is the management practice of defining the objectives that AI experience systems must achieve — and the constraints within which they must operate — rather than specifying the individual actions they must take. Instead of instructing a customer service AI to "apologize when customers express frustration," the outcome-based contract specifies that "every customer who enters an interaction with a frustration signal must exit with a measurably improved emotional state, as measured by the emotional residue score, and any interaction that fails to achieve this should be escalated for human review within 24 hours."

The advantage of outcome-based contracting is that it gives AI systems the flexibility to discover interaction strategies that humans might not have anticipated, while constraining them to operate within boundaries defined by human judgment. The disadvantage is that it requires more sophisticated measurement infrastructure — you can only contract for outcomes you can reliably measure — and more sophisticated governance processes to review whether the system is meeting its outcome objectives and operating within its ethical constraints.

Simulation as Design Tool: The Experience Sandbox

One of the most powerful capabilities enabled by the experience-as-code paradigm is the ability to test proposed experience designs against simulated customer populations before deploying them to real customers. The experience sandbox is a computational environment in which AI-based customer models — digital twins of representative customer segments — can be exposed to proposed experience designs and their likely responses observed and measured without any real customer being affected.

The experience sandbox enables a category of innovation that was not previously possible: rapid, low-risk experimentation with experience designs that might be too risky or too expensive to test in live environments. A proposed redesign of the payment flow at Stage 6, for example, might involve enough interaction complexity that a live A/B test would require weeks or months to achieve statistical significance. In the experience sandbox, the same test can be run against 10,000 customer digital twins in minutes, with confidence intervals that, while not perfectly equivalent to live test data, provide a reliable enough signal to guide the decision about whether to proceed with live testing.

Hypothetical Case Study: nHulu's Quantum Content Delivery

In 2030, nHulu deployed what internal teams called "quantum content delivery" — an event-driven experience pipeline that managed every element of the subscriber experience as code, from content recommendations to subscription management to customer service interactions. The system integrated viewing behavior data, device usage patterns, household composition signals, and payment history into a continuously updated customer model that governed every automated interaction. The outcomes were striking: subscriber churn dropped 23% in the first year of full deployment, average session length increased 18%, and the volume of inbound customer service contacts decreased 31% as proactive interventions resolved issues before customers needed to report them. The most instructive element of the nHulu case is not the outcome metrics — it is the governance architecture. nHulu created a dedicated AI Ethics and Experience team whose mandate was to continuously audit the system's decision logic, identify interventions that produced short-term engagement metrics at the cost of long-term subscriber welfare, and adjust the outcome contracts governing the system to ensure that long-term relationship health remained the primary optimization objective.

The Actionable Feedback Loop: Closing the Experience Engineering Cycle

The experience-as-code pipeline is not a one-time deployment — it is a continuously evolving system that must be regularly reviewed, updated, and improved. The feedback loop that drives this evolution is the most important process in the Customer Sensor Mesh organization: the systematic capture, analysis, and actuation of insights from every interaction across the matrix.

The feedback loop operates at four levels:

1. Real-time feedback: Individual interaction outcomes are captured immediately and fed into the A/B testing framework. Treatment protocols showing significantly above or below expected performance trigger automated notifications for review.
2. Daily feedback: Aggregate performance metrics across the matrix are reviewed. Cells showing unusual patterns — sudden drops in conversion, spikes in emotional distress signals, anomalous dwell time patterns — are investigated by the experience analytics team.
3. Weekly feedback: Predictive model accuracy is assessed against observed outcomes. Models that are drifting from their calibration are retrained or flagged for architectural review.
4. Monthly and quarterly feedback: The strategic alignment of the experience pipeline is reviewed. Are the outcome objectives the system is optimizing for still aligned with business strategy and customer values? Have competitive dynamics shifted in ways that require new capabilities or different priorities?

Building the Event-Driven Customer Experience Pipeline: Technical Architecture Guide

The experience-as-code philosophy requires a specific technical architecture — one that is fundamentally different from the batch-oriented, campaign-driven systems that most organizations have inherited from the pre-Sensor era. This section provides a technical architecture guide for Customer Experience Engineers and their technology partners building event-driven customer experience pipelines.

PART III: THE NINE REQUIREMENTS IN EVERY CUSTOMER INTERACTION

Now With AI, Sensor Networks, and Network Effects

CHAPTER EIGHT

The 9 Outcome Objectives

Required in Every Interaction — Now With AI and the Customer Sensor Mesh

The Economics of Every Customer Glance and Surface Touch

The original CxC Matrix established that every customer interaction, regardless of how brief or apparently trivial, should be designed to accomplish nine core treatment objectives. These objectives — Identify, Recognize, Fulfill, Upgrade, Cross-Sell, Expand, Educate, Collect, and Generate Referrals — form the complete vocabulary of customer relationship management.

In the Customer Sensor economy, this principle extends to the full range of micro, nano, and quantum-level interactions that sensor systems enable. A customer's biometric signal is a nano-slot interaction. The Customer Sensor Mesh system's interpretation and response to that signal is a micro-slot interaction. Both must be designed with the 9 Objectives framework — not just the macro-level interactions that traditional CX management focuses on.

Objective 1: Identify — The Quantum Recognition Challenge

Identification in the Customer Sensor Mesh era extends far beyond account authentication. The question "who is this customer?" has expanded to encompass the customer's current context: their location, device, time constraints, emotional state, immediate intent, and most likely next action. The Customer Sensor Mesh system that correctly identifies a customer as "Sarah Chen, returning customer, current context: commuting, time pressure: high, recent purchase: competing product, emotional state: slightly frustrated" is equipped to serve her dramatically better than a system that merely recognizes her account number.

The four dimensions of identification in the Matrix 3.0 are: Identity: who they are, State: how they are right now, Intent: what they are trying to accomplish, and Context: the external circumstances shaping this interaction. Achieving all four dimensions of identification simultaneously — and integrating them into a coherent picture of the customer's current reality — is the foundational requirement of the Customer Sensor Mesh experience.

Objective 2: Recognize — Beyond Personalization, Pre-Curation

Recognition means demonstrating to customers that you know them — their history, preferences, patterns, and relationship with your organization. In the pre-Sensor era, recognition was primarily expressed through personalized greetings, recommended products based on purchase history, and the retention of account information across sessions.

In the Customer Sensor Mesh era, recognition extends to pre-curation: designing the experience the customer is about to have based on who they are before they have consciously formed their request. Pre-curation means that when a loyal customer opens your app at 7:30 AM on a weekday, they see an interface optimized for their observed morning routine — not a generic homepage. It means that when a customer arrives at a retail location, the store's ambient intelligence system begins adjusting to their known preferences before they have said a word to a human employee. It means that their AI agent, arriving on their behalf at your digital interface, is greeted with a protocol optimized for their specific permission level and preference profile.

Objective 3: Fulfill — Anticipatory Satisfaction

Fulfillment means satisfying the customer's need — giving them what they came for. In the Customer Sensor economy, the leading edge of fulfillment is anticipatory: satisfying needs before customers explicitly request fulfillment. Neil's vehicle service appointment was fulfilled before he was aware of the need. Lin Wei's sparkling water was offered before she consciously chose to try it.

Anticipatory fulfillment requires a fundamental shift in how organizations think about customer service. Traditional service models are reactive: customers experience a need, express it, and the organization responds. Anticipatory service models are proactive: the organization detects a need signal before the customer has consciously formed the need, and initiates the fulfillment process without waiting to be asked. This shift from reactive to proactive requires both the sensor infrastructure to detect early-stage need signals and the operational agility to respond before the need becomes urgent or, worse, becomes a complaint.

Objective 4: Upgrade — The At-a-Glance Nudge Architecture

The upgrade objective is about expanding the customer's relationship with the organization to higher-value tiers — more features, more services, more engagement. In the

Customer Sensor Mesh framework, upgrade nudges are designed at the nano and micro-slot level: brief, non-intrusive reminders of what higher-tier customers receive, triggered at the moments when behavioral and sensor signals indicate the customer is most receptive.

The ethics of upgrade nudging in the Customer Sensor era require careful attention. The Customer Sensor Mesh system has unprecedented knowledge of customer psychological states, attention levels, and decision-making patterns. Using this knowledge to time upgrade nudges for moments of maximum customer vulnerability — when a customer is tired, stressed, or cognitively depleted — may be technically effective in the short term but is ethically problematic and strategically counterproductive. Customers who feel manipulated, even if they cannot precisely identify the mechanism, become actively hostile to the brand that manipulated them.

Objective	Traditional Implementation	Customer Sensor Enhancement	Key Metric
1. Identify	Account login / cookie tracking	Multi-dimensional state identification including emotional context	Identification accuracy across all 4 dimensions
2. Recognize	Personalized greeting / recommendations	Pre-curated experience based on predicted current state	Customer-perceived recognition score
3. Fulfill	Responding to explicit requests	Anticipatory fulfillment before conscious need expression	Anticipation accuracy rate
4. Upgrade	Upsell prompts based on purchase history	State-optimized nudge architecture at receptivity peaks	Upgrade conversion at ethical trigger moments
5. Cross-Sell	Related product recommendations	Ecosystem-aware bundling across customer's full sensor network	Cross-sell attachment rate
6. Expand	New category introduction	Adjacent-need prediction using behavioral and biometric signals	New category trial rate
7. Educate	Feature tours and help content	'You are here' customer-future movie — predictive value demonstration	Education-to-action conversion rate
8. Collect	Forms and surveys	Ethical ambient data collection with explicit value exchange	Data quality score
9. Generate Referrals	Referral program prompts	Network monetization — detecting and amplifying natural	Organic referral velocity

Objective	Traditional Implementation	Customer Sensor Enhancement	Key Metric
		advocacy moments	

The 9 Objectives in Detail: A Practitioner's Guide

Each of the 9 treatment objectives requires specific implementation strategies in the Customer Sensor Mesh environment. The following sections provide detailed guidance for implementing each objective across the four cognitive processing layers of the CxC Matrix 3.0.

Objective 5: Cross-Sell — Every Contact Is a Platform for Holistic Customer Leverage

Cross-selling in the Customer Sensor era has been transformed from a sales technique into an anticipatory service function. The traditional cross-sell was a product recommendation based on purchase history: "customers who bought X also bought Y." This approach treats cross-selling as a revenue extraction technique — a way to get more money from a customer who is already buying.

The Customer Sensor Mesh approach treats cross-selling as a customer value expansion technique — a way to provide more value to a customer by connecting them with products and services that genuinely serve their needs, identified through multi-signal data analysis rather than simplistic purchase correlation. The Customer Sensor Mesh system that observes a customer using their fitness tracking wearable intensively, notes that their usage patterns suggest they are training for a specific event, detects from their calendar data that a major athletic event is eight weeks away, and suggests relevant training equipment, nutritional products, and professional coaching services is not cross-selling in the traditional sense. It is anticipatory value delivery.

The ethics of cross-selling in the Customer Sensor Mesh environment require careful attention. The same data richness that enables genuinely helpful cross-sell suggestions also enables manipulation — surfacing offers at moments of peak vulnerability, creating artificial urgency, exploiting emotional states detected through biometric monitoring. The Customer Worthy organization designs its cross-sell protocols explicitly to maximize customer value rather than short-term revenue, recognizing that these objectives are aligned in the long term even when they diverge in any given interaction.

Objective 6: Expand — Customer Enrichment Beyond the Moment

Expansion objectives in the CxC Matrix address the longer arc of the customer relationship — the movement from initial purchase to category ownership, from single-product customer to brand ecosystem participant, from transactional relationship to valued partnership. The distinction between expansion and cross-selling is primarily temporal and strategic: cross-selling operates at the level of the individual interaction, expanding a specific purchase or solving an immediate adjacent need. Expansion operates at the level of the relationship, developing the customer's engagement with the brand over months and years.

In the Customer Sensor Mesh environment, expansion planning is informed by trajectory analysis — the use of longitudinal behavioral data and predictive modeling to identify each customer's likely evolution over time and design proactive touchpoints that support and accelerate that evolution. A customer who has been using an entry-level software subscription for six months, whose usage patterns show progressive feature adoption and increasing organizational integration, and whose job role data suggests they have recently been promoted to a position with more direct authority over technology purchasing decisions, is a customer whose expansion trajectory is visible in the data. The organization that recognizes this trajectory and invests in the relationship at the right moment — before the customer has formally begun evaluating alternatives — wins the expansion. The organization that waits for the customer to express expansion interest loses it at an expensive point of competition.

Objective 7: Educate — "You Are Here": Playing the Customer-Future Movie

The education objective in the CxC Matrix is fundamentally about value visibility: ensuring that customers can clearly see the value they are receiving from their relationship with the organization, and can clearly envision the value they could receive by deepening that relationship. This sounds straightforward but is operationally demanding, because value is often invisible.

The hours saved by an automated workflow, the risk avoided by a security system that detected a threat the user never saw, the health outcome improved by a wellness program whose benefits accumulate gradually over months — these are forms of value that require deliberate surfacing. The customer who cannot see the value their product is delivering is a customer who will undervalue their relationship, become vulnerable to competitive offers that promise equivalent or greater visible value, and eventually churn despite being objectively well-served.

The "Customer-Future Movie" concept addresses this by showing customers not just what they have received but what they will receive: a projected value trajectory that makes the long-term benefits of the relationship visible before they are fully realized. This is analogous to a financial advisor showing a client not just their current portfolio value but its projected growth trajectory — making the invisible visible, and creating commitment to a future state that the customer can now see clearly.

> **Education Objective: AI Prompt Design Principles**
>
> Education interactions in the Customer Sensor Mesh framework should satisfy four criteria: (1) They must show the customer something genuinely new — information they didn't already know about the value they are receiving or could receive. (2) They must be timed to moments when the customer is in a receptive state — not when they are task-focused on something else. (3) They must be personally relevant — not generic feature tours but specific demonstrations of value based on this customer's actual usage patterns and goals. (4) They must include a clear pathway to the next level — "here is what you're getting now, and here is what you could get by taking this specific next step." Education interactions that satisfy all four criteria consistently show conversion rates 3-5x higher than generic product communications.

Objective 8: Collect — Customer Sensing and Ethical Data Harvesting

The collection objective in the original CxC Matrix referred to information collection — gathering feedback, behavioral data, and explicit preference information that would improve future interactions. In the Customer Sensor Mesh framework, collection has expanded to encompass the full range of sensor data that the permission architecture allows the organization to gather.

The ethical dimensions of collection have become correspondingly more complex. The principle of minimum necessary data collection — gathering only what is genuinely required for the customer benefit being delivered — becomes critical when the available data stream is nearly unlimited. Organizations that collect data because they can, rather than because they have a clear use case that benefits the customer, are building compliance risk, trust deficits, and competitive vulnerability simultaneously.

The most sophisticated organizations in the Customer Sensor economy approach collection as a value exchange negotiation rather than a data extraction exercise. They articulate clearly, for each data type they collect: what specific customer benefit is enabled by this data, what the customer's alternative to sharing this data is - typically, a less personalized experience, and what control the customer has over the use, storage, and deletion of this data. Organizations that approach collection with this transparency consistently achieve higher permission levels — and therefore access to higher-quality, more complete data — than organizations that bury their collection practices in terms-of-service documents.

Objective 9: Generate Referrals — Network Monetization and Membership

The referral objective is the final stage of the CxC Matrix treatment objectives and the one most intimately connected to the Customer Sensor Mesh ecosystem as a whole. Referrals are the outcome of customers who feel so genuinely valued, so authentically served, and so clearly better off for their relationship with the organization that they voluntarily bring others into that relationship. They are not the result of referral programs, though well-designed programs can make the act of referring easier. They are the result of the entirety of the customer experience across all 14 preceding stages and all 6 channels.

In the Customer Sensor Mesh environment, referral generation has become both more automated and more genuine. More automated because behavioral signals can now identify the specific moments when a customer's advocacy impulse is at its peak — immediately after a successfully resolved service interaction, after achieving a significant milestone with a product, after receiving unexpected value from a feature they hadn't known existed — and trigger frictionless referral pathways at exactly those moments. More genuine because the Customer Sensor Mesh framework, by improving the quality of every preceding interaction, creates customers who have genuinely more to be enthusiastic about.

Referral Trigger Signal	Optimal Response Timing	Referral Format	Expected Conversion
Achievement milestone (e.g., 100 hours saved, $5,000 ROI reached)	Within 60 seconds of milestone event	Personalized milestone share with pre-drafted social message	12-18%
First successful use of advanced feature	Within 24 hours of activation	Email with "share how you're using X" prompt	8-12%

Referral Trigger Signal	Optimal Response Timing	Referral Format	Expected Conversion
Exceptional service recovery	Within 2 hours of resolution	Personal outreach from account team with referral offer	15-25%
Completed onboarding journey	Day 30 of use	Community invitation + peer introduction	10-14%
Unprompted positive social mention	Within 2 hours of detection	Amplification support + formal referral program invitation	20-35%

The Nine Objectives Matrix: Full 90-Cell Application Guide

The following table maps all nine treatment objectives across all 15 lifecycle stages, identifying which objectives are most critical at each stage and providing the primary implementation priority for the Customer Sensor environment. This mapping provides the operational foundation for the CxC Matrix cell design process.

Stage	Primary Objectives	Secondary Objectives	CS Enhancement	Key Metric
1 Awareness	Identify (context)	Educate	Machine awareness via API; algorithmic discovery optimization	Impression-to-consideration rate
2 Information	Educate, Recognize	Identify (intent)	AI-curated content	Information quality

Stage	Primary Objectives	Secondary Objectives	CS Enhancement	Key Metric
			delivery; machine-readable information architecture	score; next-step conversion
3 Identification	Identify (full), Recognize	Fulfill (informational)	Multi-dimensional identification; preference inference; contextual profiling	Identification accuracy across 4 dimensions
4 Selection	Fulfill, Recognize	Upgrade, Cross-Sell	Dynamic configuration; contextual offer assembly; comparison facilitation	Shortlist conversion rate; configuration accuracy
5 Negotiation	Fulfill, Upgrade	Cross-Sell, Expand	Agent-to-agent negotiation; transparent value presentation; trust signaling	Deal velocity; deal value; competitive win rate
6 Contract	Fulfill, Collect	Identify (verification)	Friction elimination; smart contracts; biometric verification	Cart abandonment rate; contract cycle time
7 Logistics	Fulfill, Educate	Recognize	Predictive positioning; benefit-start	On-time delivery rate;

Stage	Primary Objectives	Secondary Objectives	CS Enhancement	Key Metric
			optimization; timeline transparency	benefit-start gap
8 Delivery	Fulfill, Recognize	Educate, Collect	Dynamic service tier; acceptance experience design; first-use coaching	Delivery quality score; first-use activation rate
9 Acceptance	Educate, Collect	Generate Referrals	Shareability design; onboarding intelligence; community moment creation	Onboarding completion; Day-1 NPS; social share rate
10 Payment	Fulfill, Collect	Expand	Payment optimization; data-value exchange; tokenized loyalty	Payment friction score; alternative payment utilization
11 Use	Fulfill, Expand	Upgrade, Educate	Usage intelligence; value visibility; anticipatory benefit delivery	Feature activation depth; autonomous value delivery rate
12 Care/Support	Recognize, Fulfill	Educate, Collect	Anticipatory care; emotional calibration; proactive	Anticipation accuracy; emotional residue

Stage	Primary Objectives	Secondary Objectives	CS Enhancement	Key Metric
			resolution	score; FCR
13 Repair	Fulfill, Recognize	Generate Referrals	Predictive maintenance; heroic recovery; advocacy activation	Recovery NPS; post-repair advocacy rate
14 Disposal	Fulfill, Generate Referrals	Collect	Circular economy integration; responsible disposition; upgrade facilitation	Disposal experience score; repurchase rate
15 Community	Generate Referrals, Expand	Collect, Educate	Advocacy moment detection; network monetization; trust graph building	Referral conversion rate; community influence score

The Interaction Economics Model: Calculating Cell-Level ROI

One of the most powerful capabilities of the CxC Matrix is the ability to calculate the economic value of each cell — and therefore to make explicit, evidence-based decisions about where to invest in Customer Sensor capabilities. The Interaction Economics Model provides the framework for this calculation.

For each cell (Stage × Channel), the model calculates five economic parameters:

1. Cost per Interaction (CPI): The total cost of delivering all interactions in this cell, divided by the number of interactions. Includes technology costs, human labor costs, and overhead allocations.
2. Revenue Contribution per Interaction (RCPI): The direct revenue attributable to interactions in this cell, including new revenue generated, churn revenue prevented, and upsell/cross-sell revenue enabled.
3. Lifetime Value Contribution per Interaction (LVCPI): The indirect lifetime value impact of interactions in this cell — the change in predicted customer lifetime value attributable to the quality of interactions in this cell, measured through longitudinal customer tracking.
4. Opportunity Cost per Interaction (OCPI): The revenue that is not being captured because of suboptimal performance in this cell — the difference between current RCPI+LVCPI and the best achievable RCPI+LVCPI based on benchmark data and optimization analysis.
5. Customer Experience Value per Interaction (CXVPI): The net value delivered to the customer per interaction — a measure of how much better off the customer is as a result of the interaction, assessed through outcome data and customer feedback.

The Net Cell Value (NCV) formula combines these parameters:

NCV = (RCPI + LVCPI - CPI) × Volume + CXVPI × Trust Equity Multiplier - OCPI

The Trust Equity Multiplier reflects the fact that customer experience quality has compounding effects on trust, and trust has compounding effects on future economic outcomes. Organizations that invest in genuine customer value creation in each cell build trust equity that amplifies the economic returns of all future interactions — making the real economic value of excellent customer experience higher than any single-period measurement captures.

CHAPTER NINE

The Customer Sensor Mesh Schematic

Digital Twins, Living Blueprints, and the Architecture of Anticipatory Experience

From Customer Lifecycle Maps to Play-Forward Movies

The traditional customer lifecycle map is a spatial document: it shows where customers are at different stages of their relationship with an organization, depicted as positions in a journey with a beginning, middle, and end. This spatial metaphor was enormously useful for organizations whose customer experience management practices were largely intuitive — it made the customer journey visible, discussable, and manageable.

The Customer Sensor Mesh Schematic is something fundamentally different. It is a temporal document — not a map of where customers are, but a model of where they are going, when they will arrive, and what they will need when they get there. It is a "play-forward movie" of each customer's relationship trajectory, generated in real time by integrating current sensor signals with historical behavioral patterns and predictive models.

The most important characteristic of the Customer Sensor Mesh Schematic is that it is living: it updates continuously as new signals arrive, revising its predictions in light of new evidence. A static lifecycle map shows a customer moving from Awareness to Information to Selection in a predictable sequence. A living Customer Sensor Mesh Schematic might show that a specific customer is simultaneously advancing in three lifecycle stages (their purchase intent is increasing rapidly), retreating in two others (their satisfaction with existing service has just dropped), and experiencing a critical risk event in a fourth (they just visited a competitor's website for the first time). The schematic updates the probability distribution of this customer's future trajectory in real time and triggers appropriate interventions for each dimension simultaneously.

Building Digital Twin Schematics Addressing All Customer Dimensions

A digital twin, in the Customer Sensor Mesh context, is a continuously updated computational model of a specific customer that simulates their behavioral patterns, preference structures, emotional response profiles, and decision-making tendencies with sufficient accuracy to be used as a planning and optimization tool.

The digital twin is not a simple data record or a demographic profile. It is a dynamic simulation model that can be "run forward" to predict how a customer will respond to different interventions under different conditions. It can be used to test proposed changes to customer experience design without exposing real customers to the potentially negative consequences of failed experiments. And it can be used to identify the personalized intervention that will most effectively move a specific customer toward a desired outcome — a precision that population-level A/B testing cannot achieve.

The architecture of the Customer Sensor Schematic digital twin has five layers:

1. Identity Constellation Layer: The persistent, stable attributes of the customer — demographic information, long-term preference patterns, core values and priorities, relationship history with the organization.
2. Intent Prediction Layer: The real-time inference of the customer's current motivations, immediate goals, and short-horizon intentions based on recent behavioral signals.
3. Emotional State Layer: The continuous assessment of the customer's current emotional state and trajectory based on biometric signals, interaction patterns, and contextual factors.
4. Value Optimization Layer: The calculation, in real time, of the optimal treatment protocol for this customer at this moment — the action most likely to advance both customer outcomes and business objectives simultaneously.
5. Action Orchestration Layer: The selection, sequencing, and delivery of interventions across all relevant channels and devices, coordinated by the value optimization calculation.

Digital Twin Design Principles

A customer digital twin is only as valuable as the accuracy of its underlying models. Three principles guide effective twin design: (1) Transparency — customers should understand that a digital twin model exists, have access to the data it uses, and be able to correct inaccuracies. (2) Representativeness — the twin should represent the customer's actual values and preferences, not the organization's preferred interpretation of them. (3) Humility — the twin should acknowledge its own uncertainty, flagging predictions with low confidence rather than presenting all outputs with equal authority. Twins built on these principles generate significantly higher customer permission levels than those that operate as black boxes.

The Customer Sensor Schematic as Organizational Asset

The Customer Sensor Schematic — the complete system of digital twin models, predictive trajectory models, and simulation environments — represents one of the most valuable organizational assets in the Customer Sensor economy. It embodies the organization's accumulated understanding of its customers: their behavioral patterns, their preference structures, their response to different interaction designs, and their trajectories across the customer lifecycle.

Unlike most organizational assets, the Customer Sensor Schematic improves continuously without direct investment — because every customer interaction generates outcome data that refines the underlying models. An organization that has been building and maintaining its Customer Sensor Schematic for five years has a customer intelligence asset that a new entrant would take years to replicate, regardless of the new entrant's technology investment. The compounding advantage of accumulated behavioral data and refined predictive models is the most powerful form of the network effect in the Customer Sensor economy.

The governance of the Customer Sensor Schematic as an organizational asset requires the same rigor applied to financial and intellectual property assets. The Schematic should have a defined owner (typically the Chief Experience

Officer or Chief Data Officer), a clear data retention and refresh policy, a security architecture that protects against both external breach and internal misuse, and a customer transparency framework that ensures individuals have access to understand and correct their own digital twin representations.

Digital Twin Accuracy Assessment

Organizations should regularly assess the accuracy of their digital twin models against observed customer behavior. Key accuracy metrics include: Prediction Accuracy Rate (what percentage of model predictions match observed outcomes within 20% margin?), Segment Representation Coverage (what percentage of active customers have digital twin models with sufficient behavioral data for reliable predictions?), Model Drift Rate (how quickly does model accuracy degrade without retraining, as customer behavior evolves?), and Demographic Accuracy Parity (is prediction accuracy consistent across demographic groups, or does the model perform significantly better for some groups than others?). Models that score poorly on any of these metrics should be retrained, redesigned, or deprecated rather than used to drive customer interactions.

CHAPTER TEN

The Customer's Ecosystem

Networks of Trust, AI Agents, and the Preparing for the Algorithmic Customer

The Rise of the Customer Operating System

By 2031, every connected consumer will operate through what industry analysts are beginning to call a Customer Operating System — a coordinated platform of AI agents, data management tools, and autonomous negotiation capabilities that allows individuals to manage their entire marketplace relationship portfolio with minimal direct cognitive investment.

The Customer OS is not a single application from a single vendor. It is an ecosystem of interoperating services: a financial management system that tracks all spending and models future scenarios, a health management system that monitors wellness metrics and manages care relationships, a home management system that oversees maintenance, utilities, and consumer goods procurement, a mobility system that manages transportation relationships, and a communications system that manages professional and personal correspondence. These services share data with appropriate privacy controls, coordinate autonomous actions within established permission frameworks, and report to the customer through a unified interface.

For companies, the emergence of the Customer OS creates a new primary customer to serve: not just the human consumer, but the AI agents acting on their behalf.

Organizations that make their offerings accessible, evaluable, and negotiable through the Customer OS infrastructure will have access to customers who have largely delegated marketplace interaction to autonomous systems. Those that do not will find themselves increasingly invisible to the growing share of customer needs that are managed autonomously.

Preparing for the Algorithmic Customer

The algorithmic customer — a customer whose interactions with your organization are primarily or entirely mediated by AI systems — requires a fundamentally different service architecture than the human customer. Five dimensions of the service architecture must be reconceived:

Architecture Dimension	Human Customer Design	Algorithmic Customer Design
Discovery	SEO, advertising, brand awareness	Machine-readable product catalogs, API-first offering description, structured negotiation protocols
Evaluation	Product pages, reviews, demos	Standardized performance data feeds, verifiable third-party benchmarks, simulation-ready product models
Negotiation	Pricing pages, promotional offers	Dynamic pricing APIs, automated discount qualification, real-time availability confirmation
Transaction	Checkout flow, payment processing	Bot-to-bot transaction APIs, smart contract execution, automated compliance verification
Post-purchase	Onboarding, support, renewal	Autonomous usage optimization, predictive maintenance alerts,

Architecture Dimension	Human Customer Design	Algorithmic Customer Design
		proactive renewal negotiation

The Trust Economy, Bad Actors, and Catastrophic Damage

The expansion of AI-mediated customer experience creates profound trust vulnerabilities that did not exist in human-mediated service environments. In a human service interaction, trust is built and validated through behavioral signals that humans have evolved over millennia to interpret: tone of voice, facial expression, body language, the track record of personal relationships. These signals are difficult to fake at scale.

In AI-mediated environments, trust must be verified through different mechanisms: algorithmic transparency, auditable decision logic, verifiable performance data, and cryptographic authentication. The absence of these mechanisms creates attack surfaces that bad actors are already beginning to exploit — from deepfake impersonation of customer service agents to algorithmic manipulation of comparison platforms to prompt injection attacks on customer AI agents.

Organizations that invest in trust infrastructure — transparent AI systems, verifiable performance metrics, cryptographic identity validation, and customer-controlled data governance — are building the most durable form of competitive advantage available in the algorithmic economy. Trust, once lost in an AI-mediated environment, is extraordinarily difficult to rebuild. The reputational damage from a single high-profile algorithmic failure — a pricing system that systematically disadvantaged protected groups, an AI agent that was manipulated into recommending competitor products, a biometric data breach — can be existential for organizations that have not built trust into their foundational architecture.

Building the Trust Architecture: A Practical Framework

Trust in the Customer Sensor economy is not a feeling — it is an architecture. It is a system of verifiable commitments, transparent processes, auditable decisions, and customer-controlled governance that gives customers concrete reasons to grant the permission levels that enable the best Customer Sensor experiences. The organizations that build genuine trust architecture will have sustainable competitive advantages that are extremely difficult to replicate, because trust infrastructure is expensive and slow to build and can be destroyed instantly by a single high-profile failure.

The Four Pillars of Customer Sensor Trust

Pillar 1: Transparency — Making the Invisible Visible

Transparency in the Customer Sensor context means giving customers clear, accessible, honest information about what data the organization collects about them, how that data is used, what automated decisions are made based on that data, and what the customer's options are for controlling or exiting the data relationship. This is more demanding than regulatory compliance transparency — it goes beyond providing technically accurate disclosures in terms-of-service documents to genuinely helping customers understand their relationship with the organization's data systems.

The gold standard of Customer Sensor transparency is the Customer Data Dashboard: an interface that gives each customer a complete, real-time view of their own data within the organization's systems. This dashboard shows what data is collected and from what sources, how that data has been used in automated decisions that affected the customer, what the customer's current permission grants are and how to change them, and what the data retention schedule is for each data type. Organizations that have deployed customer-facing data dashboards consistently report higher permission levels and lower churn among dashboard users than non-users — because transparency builds trust rather than undermining it.

Pillar 2: Control — Genuine Agency Over the Data Relationship

Control means that customers have real, practical, low-friction options for managing their data relationship with the organization — not just theoretical rights that are technically accessible but practically difficult to exercise. Genuine control architecture includes:

- Granular consent management: customers can grant or revoke consent for each data type independently, in real time, through a simple interface, without affecting other parts of their service relationship
- Purpose limitation enforcement: data collected for one explicitly stated purpose is not repurposed without explicit additional consent — and the system enforces this limitation technically rather than relying on policy compliance

- Data portability: customers can export their data in machine-readable format, enabling them to take it to competing services and enabling the market mechanisms that reward organizations that use data well
- Right to erasure: customers who want to end their data relationship with the organization can do so cleanly — their data is deleted, their inferences are purged, and the organization's systems return to a genuinely blank slate

Pillar 3: Accountability — Demonstrable Responsibility

Accountability means that the organization can demonstrate — to customers, regulators, and the public — that its data practices are consistent with its commitments. This requires more than policy: it requires auditable systems, verifiable compliance records, and third-party validation.

The most credible accountability infrastructure combines internal controls (algorithmic auditing, privacy impact assessments, regular compliance reviews) with external validation (third-party privacy audits, regulatory certification programs, independent ethics reviews). Organizations that actively seek external accountability validation and publish the results are demonstrably more trustworthy than those that rely on self-certification — and in the Customer Sensor era, demonstrable trustworthiness is a competitive differentiator that influences customer permission grants and purchase decisions.

Pillar 4: Value Exchange — Making the Trade Worth Making

The final pillar of trust architecture is the most often neglected: ensuring that the value the customer receives from the data relationship is genuinely proportionate to the data and permission they provide. This is not just an ethical requirement — it is a commercial one. Customers who feel that they receive good value from their data relationships with organizations grant more permissions, share more data, and are more loyal than customers who feel that the value exchange is one-sided.

The value exchange calculation varies by data type and use case. Location data that enables convenience (navigation, nearby store information, delivery optimization) has a clear, tangible value proposition. Emotional state data that enables more appropriate service interactions has a real but less tangible value proposition. Physiological health data that enables predictive health management has a potentially high-stakes value proposition. The organization's job is to make the value proposition for each data type legible and credible — and to ensure that the customer benefit genuinely materializes rather than remaining theoretical.

Game Theory and Multi-Agent Trust Systems

The emergence of AI agents as participants in trust relationships creates a new dimension of trust complexity. When a customer's AI agent grants permission to a company's AI system on the customer's behalf, the trust relationship is mediated — the customer trusts their agent, and the agent evaluates the company's trustworthiness and makes permission decisions accordingly.

For companies, this creates an opportunity and a risk. The opportunity: well-designed, transparent, auditable AI systems that clearly communicate their data practices in machine-readable formats will receive higher permission levels from customer agents than opaque or misleading systems. The risk: customer agents that discover a discrepancy between a company's stated data practices and its actual behavior will not just revoke permissions — they will flag the company as untrustworthy in the trust graphs that customer agents share with each other. A trust failure in the agent economy propagates faster and more systematically than a trust failure in the human economy.

Trust graphs — networks of shared trust assessments maintained by customer AI agents — are an emerging infrastructure for managing trust in the algorithmic economy. In their nascent form today, these are simple reputation systems: AI assistants that remember that a certain company's AI agent made false claims or attempted manipulation during a previous negotiation. By 2031, trust graphs will be more formalized: structured data systems that record trust assessment evidence, weight assessments by the credibility of the assessing agent, and propagate trust assessments through the agent network to inform future decisions.

Designing for the Algorithmic Customer: A Practitioner's Guide

The emergence of the algorithmic customer — a customer whose interactions with your organization are primarily or entirely mediated by AI agents — is the single most significant structural change in commercial relationships since the Internet. Organizations that design effectively for algorithmic customers will have sustainable advantages in efficiency, scale, and relationship depth. Organizations that do not will find themselves progressively marginalized in categories where automation rates are high.

Making Your Organization Machine-Readable

The most important practical step in designing for the algorithmic customer is making your organization machine-readable — ensuring that every aspect of your offering that an AI agent would need to evaluate, compare, and transact can be accessed programmatically with high quality, high reliability, and low latency.

Machine readability encompasses several specific capabilities that must be designed and maintained. Product and service catalog APIs provide structured, queryable access to your full offering, with standardized attribute schemas that allow agents to compare your offerings against competitors on consistent dimensions. Pricing transparency APIs provide real-time, accurate pricing information including all fees, terms conditions, and available discount structures — not the simplified "starting at" pricing that characterizes many human-facing product pages. Performance certification feeds provide verifiable third-party data on product or service performance metrics — not self-reported marketing claims but independently validated evidence that an agent can assess objectively. Availability and fulfillment APIs provide real-time inventory, delivery capability, and service slot availability that agents need to make accurate purchase recommendations.

The MCP Ecosystem: Model Context Protocol in Practice

The Model Context Protocol (MCP) is the emerging standard for machine-to-machine communication in commercial contexts — the protocol that allows customer AI agents to discover, evaluate, and transact with company AI systems in a standardized, secure, and auditable way. Understanding MCP and designing your AI systems for effective MCP participation is as strategically important today as having a coherent SEO strategy was in 2005 — and organizations that are not investing in MCP capability are accumulating a competitive debt that will become increasingly expensive to repay as MCP adoption accelerates.

MCP participation requires several organizational investments. First, an MCP-compliant product catalog that exposes your offering in standardized machine-readable formats. Second, authentication and security infrastructure that allows agent-to-agent transactions to be verified and protected against fraud and manipulation. Third, negotiation protocol design that defines what terms are negotiable through automated channels, what parameters govern each negotiation, and how disputes or edge cases are escalated to human review. Fourth, logging and audit infrastructure that records all agent-to-agent interactions for compliance, quality management, and customer transparency purposes.

Protecting Against Algorithmic Customer Exploitation

The same infrastructure that enables efficient, trustworthy algorithmic customer service also creates potential vulnerabilities to exploitation by malicious agents. As automated purchasing increases in volume, so does the financial incentive to build agents designed to exploit weaknesses in company AI systems — agents that use prompt injection attacks to manipulate decision logic, agents that fabricate customer context to qualify for discounts they are not entitled to, or agents that coordinate across multiple fake customer identities to game pricing systems.

The protection architecture for algorithmic customers requires several layers of defense. Identity verification that validates the authenticity of agent claims about customer identity and permission levels. Rate limiting and anomaly detection that identifies unusual patterns of agent interaction that may indicate coordinated exploitation. Behavioral fingerprinting that distinguishes between agents representing genuine human customers and agents operating without legitimate human authorization. And audit logging that creates a complete, tamper-evident record of every agent interaction for fraud investigation and regulatory compliance purposes.

The organizations best positioned to manage these risks are those that have designed their algorithmic customer infrastructure with security as a foundational requirement rather than a retrofit. Security architecture in agent-to-agent commerce is analogous to the authentication and fraud prevention infrastructure that made e-commerce viable in the late 1990s — it is the trust infrastructure that makes the new commercial model work at scale.

PART IV: QUANTUM CUSTOMER TRANSFORMATION 2031–3038

The Long Arc of the Customer Sensor Future

CHAPTER ELEVEN

The Wearable Intelligence Era

Skin, Signal, and Sensation as Interface: 2031–2038

The Wearable Intelligence Threshold: 2031

By 2031, wearable technology will reach the Wearable Intelligence Threshold — the point at which wearable devices routinely carry sufficient processing power, battery life, sensor breadth, and AI capability to serve as primary interaction surfaces for the Customer Sensor economy. The smartphone, already a peripheral device for many users by 2030, will complete its transition from primary interface to secondary fallback. The wrist, ear, eye, and skin will become the primary channels for customer experience delivery.

The Wearable Intelligence Threshold does not represent a sudden transition. It is the culmination of a decade of progressive development: smartwatches that began as fitness trackers and progressively acquired communication, payment, and health management capabilities; earbuds that evolved from audio playback devices to ambient intelligence interfaces capable of real-time language translation, contextual information delivery, and biometric monitoring; AR glasses that moved from novelty to enterprise tool to consumer mainstream; and smart textile wearables that integrated sensor capabilities into clothing and accessories without the form factor constraints of traditional devices.

Year	Wearable Intelligence Milestone	Customer Experience Implications
2025	Mainstream health monitoring wearables; basic autonomous action capability	Early Customer Sensor mesh integration; health and wellness CX applications
2027	AR glasses reach mass-market price points; spatial computing mainstream	Physical-digital hybrid experiences become standard; ambient retail intelligence
2029	Neural interface peripherals enter consumer market; BCi-basic wearables	Thought-adjacent interaction; intent detection before vocalization
2031	Wearable Intelligence Threshold — full Customer Sensor integration	Wearables become primary CX delivery channel; sensor-first experience design
2033	Predictive wearable intelligence — anticipates needs 4-8 hours in advance	Proactive service delivery becomes standard across all major categories
2035	Neural interface wearables mainstream; thought-to-action latency <200ms	Cognitive experience design; experiences optimized for conscious processing speed
2038	Ambient wearable intelligence — always on, always optimizing, invisible	Experience design dissolves into environmental intelligence; sensor ubiquity

Designing for the Wearable-First Customer

Designing customer experiences for wearable-first customers requires a fundamental rethinking of interaction paradigms that were developed for screen-based interfaces. The constraints and affordances of wearable devices differ dramatically from those of smartphones and computers, and designs that work on a phone screen often fail completely on a watch face or an AR overlay.

The primary constraint of wearable-first design is attention scarcity. Wearable devices are used in contexts where the user's conscious attention is primarily directed elsewhere — running, commuting, working, exercising. Customer experiences delivered through wearables must be designed to be processed in peripheral or divided attention states. They must be instantly comprehensible, if they require more than 200 milliseconds to understand, they will be ignored; non-intrusive, if they interrupt the primary task, they will be resented; and immediately actionable, if they require the customer to switch contexts to respond, they will be deferred until forgotten.

These constraints push customer experience engineering design toward its most essential form: the single, clear signal that communicates maximum value in minimum time with minimum effort. This is, paradoxically, a more demanding design challenge than creating a complex, feature-rich screen-based interface. Every word, every visual element, every interaction requirement must be justified against the extreme economy of the wearable context.

The Wearable CxC Matrix: Interaction Design by Lifecycle Stage

Each of the 15 lifecycle stages in the CxC Matrix has specific wearable interaction design requirements:

Lifecycle Stage	Wearable Interaction Pattern	Optimal Signal Type
Awareness	Ambient discovery — contextual relevance alerts	Haptic pulse + voice micro-summary
Information	On-demand micro-briefings — bite-sized product data	Voice + AR overlay
Selection	Comparison shortcuts — simplified decision support	Haptic + visual indicator
Negotiation	Autonomous agent negotiation with human override	Voice confirmation + haptic approval
Contract	Biometric signature + verbal confirmation	Voice + haptic + visual confirmation
Logistics	Real-time tracking + proactive status updates	Haptic milestones + voice ETA
Delivery	Completion confirmation + quality verification	Haptic alert + visual check
Use	Usage coaching + feature discovery	Contextual voice guidance + haptic cues
Care/Support	Proactive issue detection + instant escalation	Haptic alert + voice connection
Community	Micro-advocacy moments + organic referral triggers	Voice + haptic celebration

Designing the Wearable Customer Experience: A Practitioner's Guide to 2031-2038

The Eight Interaction Primitives of Wearable Experience

Wearable device interfaces share a vocabulary of interaction primitives — fundamental interaction types that are supported across device categories and that customer experience engineer designers must master to create effective wearable experiences. Unlike screen-based interfaces, which can support arbitrarily complex interaction patterns, wearable interfaces are constrained to a small set of primitives by their form factor, the context of use, and the physiological limitations of the interaction surface.

Primitive 1: Haptic Pulse

The haptic pulse is the most universally available and contextually appropriate interaction primitive for wearable CX. A brief vibration pattern delivered to the wrist, ear canal, or other wearable contact point provides a non-intrusive, heads-up notification that something requires the wearer's attention. Haptic patterns can be differentiated by duration, intensity, rhythm, and location to communicate different information types — a single brief pulse for a low-priority notification, a triple pulse for a time-sensitive opportunity, a sustained gentle vibration for an ongoing condition requiring awareness.

The discipline of haptic design — developing meaningful, intuitive, learnable haptic languages for wearable CX — is emerging as a specialized practice within experience design. The best haptic designs are ones that customers learn without effort, because the patterns feel inherently appropriate to their content: a rapid, irregular pulse feels urgent; a slow, regular pulse feels informational. Haptic patterns that violate these intuitive mappings require explicit learning and generate friction rather than fluency.

Primitive 2: Ambient Voice

Ambient voice interaction — the ability to speak naturally with an AI system without holding a device, looking at a screen, or deliberately initiating an interaction — is perhaps the most transformative wearable interaction primitive. Through earbuds, smart glasses, or ambient room speakers, customers can interact with AI systems in the same natural way they interact with other people: speaking a request or question and receiving a response audibly.

The design challenge of ambient voice CX is managing the boundary between intended interaction and unintended activation. A customer who makes an offhand comment near an ambient voice system should not generate unintended interactions. The interaction boundary must be clearly defined — through explicit wake words, physical activation gestures, or contextual AI that can distinguish between directed communication and ambient conversation — and must be perceived by customers as reliable and controllable.

Primitive 3: Glanceable Visual

The glanceable visual is an information display that can be fully comprehended in a single brief glance — 200 milliseconds or less. This is the fundamental constraint of smartwatch display design and the primary challenge of AR overlay design: all information must be expressible in a format that can be read without sustained visual attention. Glanceable visuals are characterized by high contrast, minimal text (typically fewer than 6 words), large primary information elements, and clear visual hierarchy that directs attention to the most important information first.

The discipline of glanceable design is as much about deciding what to omit as about deciding what to include. The most effective glanceable displays communicate a single most important piece of information with maximum clarity, provide a visual indicator of whether additional information is available if the user wants it, and offer a clear call to action if one is appropriate. Everything else is noise.

The 2031 Wearable Customer Experience Scorecard

As wearable devices approach the Wearable Intelligence Threshold, organizations should assess their readiness to deliver effective wearable-first customer experiences. The following scorecard assesses five dimensions of wearable CX readiness:

Readiness Dimension	Assessment Questions	Score 1-5	Target by 2031
Content Architecture	Is your content library segmented by interaction type for wearable delivery? Do you have glanceable formats for all primary information types?		5
Haptic Language Design	Have you defined a haptic vocabulary for your customer interactions? Is it tested and validated for your customer population?		4
Voice	Do your key customer		4

Readiness Dimension	Assessment Questions	Score 1-5	Target by 2031
Interaction Design	interactions work effectively through voice-only interfaces? Are they tested for ambient use contexts?		
Permission Architecture	Can customers grant and revoke wearable data permissions independently through a wearable interface?		5
Cross-Device Continuity	Can a customer begin an interaction on a wearable and continue it seamlessly on another device without loss of context?		5

Neural Interface Wearables: Preparing for 2035

The emergence of consumer neural interface wearables — devices that can detect and interpret brain electrical activity to infer intent, attention state, and emotional valence — will represent the most profound shift in wearable CX since the smartphone. These devices are not science fiction: functional consumer-grade neural interface devices were already commercially available in research contexts by 2025, with EEG-based headbands that could detect focus states, meditation depth, and broad emotional categories.

By 2035, neural interface wearables will have improved sufficiently in accuracy, form factor, and comfort to be worn routinely by a significant portion of the engaged technology consumer population. Their CX implications are profound. A system that can detect that a customer is in a high-focus state can time educational content delivery to coincide with peak receptivity. A system that detects a customer is in a low-energy, high-stress state can hold interactions that would be poorly received until a better state arrives. A system that detects that a customer is experiencing cognitive load in a specific product decision can offer simplification assistance proactively.

The ethical constraints for neural interface CX are the most stringent of any sensing modality. Brain state data is among the most intimate personal information that exists — it directly reflects internal cognitive and emotional states that individuals may not consciously choose to share. The permission architecture for neural interface data must be the most explicit, most granular, and most revocable of any data type in the Customer Sensor ecosystem. And the use of neural interface data to influence purchasing behavior — timed to moments of neural vulnerability or optimized for neural persuasion — represents a category of manipulation that no ethical Customer Sensor organization should engage in.

Wearable Intelligence by Sector: Implementation Deep-Dives

Healthcare Wearables: The Continuous Care Platform

Healthcare wearables represent the highest-stakes deployment category for Customer Sensor Mesh capabilities. The data collected by healthcare wearables — heart rate, blood oxygen, blood pressure, glucose levels, cardiac rhythm, sleep architecture, activity intensity — is simultaneously among the most clinically valuable and most privacy-sensitive data in existence. The implications of this data for individual health outcomes can be profound and immediate.

The clinical value case for healthcare wearables is now well-established. Continuous cardiac monitoring wearables have demonstrated the ability to detect atrial fibrillation episodes that would have gone undiagnosed without continuous monitoring, enabling early treatment that prevents strokes. Continuous glucose monitors have transformed diabetes management by providing real-time glucose data that enables precise insulin dosing and lifestyle adjustment. Sleep monitoring wearables have identified sleep apnea in patients who had no prior awareness of the condition, enabling treatment that improved health outcomes across multiple dimensions.

By 2031, the Wearable Intelligence Threshold will have transformed healthcare wearables from monitoring devices into active clinical systems. Wearables that can not only detect cardiac rhythm abnormalities but autonomously alert clinical teams, share relevant data with emergency services, and even administer therapeutic interventions (anticoagulants in atrial fibrillation, insulin in hyperglycemia) will be commercially available for patients with qualifying conditions. The Customer Sensor Mesh implications of this transformation are significant: the relationship between patient, patient care circle and healthcare provider becomes a continuous, real-time partnership rather than an episodic, encounter-based transaction.

Enterprise Wearables: The Augmented Workplace

Enterprise wearable deployments — smart glasses for warehouse workers, safety wearables for construction workers, cognitive load monitors for knowledge workers — represent a growing application category for Customer Sensor principles in B2B contexts. In these applications, the "customer" is the employee using the wearable, and the "company" is both the employer and the enterprise software vendors whose applications run on the device.

The enterprise wearable value proposition is built around three pillars: safety: wearables that detect physiological indicators of fatigue, distraction, or environmental hazard before accidents occur, productivity: wearables that provide real-time guidance, information access, and process support that reduce task completion time and error rates, and health and wellbeing: wearables that monitor employee health indicators and support wellness initiatives.

The governance challenges of enterprise wearables are distinctive from consumer healthcare wearable governance because the data is collected in a workplace context where power dynamics affect the meaningfulness of consent. An employee who is asked to wear a workplace wearable as a condition of employment may technically consent but may not be doing so freely in a meaningful sense. Enterprise wearable programs that respect this dynamic — making participation genuinely voluntary, limiting data collection to the minimum necessary for the stated operational purpose, and providing employees with clear visibility into what data is collected and how it is used — achieve significantly higher employee acceptance and program effectiveness than those that treat consent as a formality.

Wearable-First Experience Design: Practical Examples Across the CxC Matrix

The following examples illustrate what wearable-first experience design looks like for each of the 15 lifecycle stages, providing concrete guidance for CX teams designing Customer Sensor experiences for wearable delivery in 2031 and beyond.

Stage	Traditional Channel Design	Wearable-First Design	Interaction Duration
Awareness	Display ad or search result	Contextual haptic + ambient voice micro-summary at moment of need relevance	<3 seconds
Information	Website or brochure	On-demand voice briefing + AR overlay comparison tool	30-90 seconds
Identification	Login/account creation form	Biometric authentication + preference sync from wearable profile	<5 seconds
Selection	Product page + comparison table	Wrist-display shortlist + voice-guided decision support	60-180 seconds
Negotiation	Chat/phone/email negotiation	Agent-to-agent with haptic approval prompt for human review	<10 seconds human time
Contract	Checkout form + confirmation	Biometric signature + haptic confirmation	<15 seconds

Stage	Traditional Channel Design	Wearable-First Design	Interaction Duration
Logistics	Email tracking updates	Proactive haptic milestones + ETA voice updates	Push only, <5 sec each
Delivery	Doorbell/delivery notification	Wrist alert + voice guidance for setup/receipt	<20 seconds
Acceptance	Email welcome/onboarding	Guided first-use experience via voice + AR overlay	5-15 minutes
Payment	Invoice/payment portal	Wrist display summary + tap-to-confirm payment	<10 seconds
Use	In-app feature discovery	Contextual voice coaching at moment of feature relevance	As needed, <30 sec each
Care/Support	Help desk contact	Proactive haptic alert + voice diagnosis before problem worsens	<60 seconds for routine
Repair	Support ticket creation	Wrist-display diagnostic + automatic appointment scheduling	<2 minutes
Disposal	Website form or store return	Wrist reminder + AR guidance for recycling/return process	<5 minutes
Community	Email referral invitation	Haptic achievement +	<10 seconds

Stage	Traditional Channel Design	Wearable-First Design	Interaction Duration
		ambient voice celebration + one-tap share	

CHAPTER TWELVE

Digitally Aware Environments

The Self-Aware Built World: 2033–3038

When Buildings Begin to Think

In 2033, the built environment will cross a threshold analogous to the Wearable Intelligence Threshold of 2031: the Built World Intelligence Threshold. At this point, commercial and residential environments routinely integrate sufficient sensor density, edge computing capacity, and AI capability to function as active participants in customer experiences rather than passive settings for them.

This transformation has been building since the first wave of building management systems in the 1980s. HVAC control systems, security cameras, access management systems, lighting controls — these were the primitive nervous systems of intelligent buildings, capable of monitoring and responding to basic environmental conditions. The addition of consumer IoT devices in the 2010s and smart building platforms in the 2020s progressively increased the sensor density and analytical capability of built environments. By 2033, the integration of edge AI, computer vision, spatial computing, and high-bandwidth mesh networking will produce buildings that can perceive, interpret, and respond to the full complexity of human presence and behavior.

Customer Experience in the Digitally Aware Environment

The customer experience implications of the digitally aware built environment are profound across every sector:

Retail: The Ambient Retail Intelligence Transformation

In the digitally aware retail environment of 2033, the store itself becomes a Customer Sensor system. Computer vision arrays monitor customer movement patterns, dwell time, engagement behavior, and emotional signals. Ambient AI systems adjust lighting, temperature, scent, and sound in real time to optimize the shopping environment for the current customer mix. Digital surface technologies transform every physical surface — shelving, flooring, display cases, fitting room mirrors — into interactive interfaces that respond to individual customer presence with personalized information, recommendations, and offers.

The retail associate's role transforms from information provider to experience curator. AI systems surface relevant customer context information on discreet wearable displays — this customer has been looking at running shoes for 12 minutes, has purchased from the brand twice before, and their behavioral signals suggest they are comparing two specific models — allowing associates to deliver consultative expertise with AI-augmented context. The result is a service interaction that combines the warmth, judgment, and relational quality of human service with the precision and personalization of AI-powered customer knowledge.

Healthcare: The Patient Sensor Environment

In the digitally aware healthcare environment, clinical sensing extends beyond the examination room. Waiting areas equipped with ambient biometric monitors can detect patients experiencing acute stress, pain escalation, or medical urgency and proactively alert clinical staff and patient care circle before the patient needs to ask for help. Smart hospital rooms continuously monitor patient vital signs and behavioral patterns, detecting early indicators of deterioration or discomfort and triggering proactive care responses. Outpatient facilities equipped with spatial analytics can identify workflow inefficiencies, guide patient and patient care circles with assistance, advice, to aid recovery and eliminate issues , obstacles, miscommunications that extend patient wait times and dynamically adjust staffing and scheduling.

Financial Services: The Intelligent Branch

By 2033, physical bank branches will have largely transformed from transaction-processing centers into consultation environments equipped with ambient intelligence. The digitally aware branch environment detects when a customer enters, calls up their relationship profile and recent account activity, identifies likely service needs based on behavioral patterns and recent account events, and pre-stages the consultation environment accordingly — the right advisor is notified and prepared, the right materials are queued, the right private room is allocated if the customer's profile indicates they typically conduct sensitive conversations.

Digitally Aware Environments: Sector-by-Sector Design Guide

Education: The Adaptive Learning Environment

The digitally aware educational environment of 2033 continuously monitors student engagement, comprehension, and emotional state to deliver personalized learning experiences that adapt in real time to each student's current needs. Ambient sensors track student attention and focus levels, identifying when individual students are confused, disengaged, or experiencing cognitive overload. AI systems interpret these signals to adjust content delivery — slowing down, providing additional scaffolding, or offering supplementary resources when a student's signals indicate comprehension difficulty.

The CxC Matrix framework applies directly to educational environments: students move through lifecycle stages from Awareness (discovering a new concept) through Information (understanding its foundations) and Selection (choosing an approach or application) through Use (practicing and applying the skill) and Community (teaching and mentoring peers). Each stage has distinct educational support requirements, and the digitally aware environment can identify which stage each student is in and provide the appropriate support automatically.

The privacy and ethical dimensions of educational sensing require especially careful attention. Students are a vulnerable population, and the data generated by educational sensing — attention levels, comprehension signals, emotional states, learning difficulties — is among the most sensitive personal data that can be collected about an individual. Educational sensing programs must be designed with minimal data collection, strict purpose limitation, robust security, and genuinely informed parent and student consent.

Hospitality: The Anticipatory Guest Experience

The hospitality sector is one of the earliest adopters of ambient intelligence for customer experience — both because the high-touch nature of hospitality makes the value of personalization obvious, and because the physical environment of hotels and resorts is particularly amenable to sensor integration. The digitally aware hotel of 2033 knows who is checking in before the guest reaches the front desk, has the room pre-configured to their known preferences, routes them to their room via their preferred path, and manages every element of their stay anticipatorily.

By 2033, this data ecosystem will be augmented with ambient sensing that detects when a guest has returned to the room, what their physiological state indicates about their current needs, and whether their behavioral patterns suggest they are working, resting, or preparing for an activity — and adjusts the room environment, surfaces relevant service options, and manages communication proactively.

Transportation: The Intelligent Mobility Experience

The digitally aware transportation experience of 2033 extends far beyond the connected vehicle of 2025. The intelligent mobility environment encompasses the full journey: the smart home environment that prepares the traveler for departure, the connected vehicle or public transit experience during travel, the smart destination environment that receives the traveler, and the return journey. Each stage of the journey is managed by ambient intelligence systems that communicate with each other and with the traveler to optimize for safety, comfort, efficiency, and personal preference simultaneously.

The transit environment of 2033 knows that a regular commuter typically boards at Stop 4 every weekday morning and exits at Stop 12. It notifies them proactively of delays that will affect their journey. It reserves their preferred seat category when possible. It manages their fare payment automatically. It provides commute-appropriate content — news, podcasts, work documents — pre-staged for their likely consumption preferences during the journey. And it coordinates with their destination environment — workplace, home, appointment — to ensure the receiving environment is prepared for their arrival.

Workplace: The Employee-Customer Experience Convergence

The distinction between customer experience and employee experience is dissolving in the digitally aware workplace. The employee is simultaneously a customer of the organization's internal services (HR, IT, facilities, communications) and a producer of the organization's external customer experiences. The quality of the employee experience directly affects the quality of the customer experience — and the digitally aware workplace is being designed to optimize both simultaneously.

Smart office environments in 2033 monitor workspace utilization, adjust environmental conditions for productivity and wellbeing, manage resource availability dynamically, and provide employees with the AI-augmented intelligence they need to serve customers effectively. The customer service representative whose workstation automatically surfaces the full customer context when a call begins, whose AI assistant can answer routine queries and suggest responses to complex ones, and whose environment adapts to support their performance during high-volume periods is an employee who can deliver a customer experience categorically better than one without these augmentations.

The Home as Customer Experience Platform

By 2033, the home will have become the most important customer experience delivery platform for most consumer-facing organizations. The proliferation of smart home devices — speakers, displays, appliances, environmental systems, security systems, health monitors — combined with the improving intelligence of home AI platforms will transform the home from a passive setting for customer experience to an active participant in delivering it.

The organizations that are most successful in the home-as-platform environment are those that design for the unique characteristics of the home context. Unlike retail or service environments, the home is the customer's private space — a context where the tolerance for commercial intrusion is low and the premium on genuine value delivery is high. Experiences that would be welcome in a retail context ("can I suggest a complementary product?") may feel intrusive in a home context. Experiences that feel robotic or transactional in a retail context may feel genuinely caring in a home context because the bar for personal relevance is higher and the expectation of relationship is stronger.

CHAPTER THIRTEEN

Self-Programming Systems

Autonomous, Self-Optimizing Customer Networks

The Five Levels of Autonomous Customer Experience

Drawing from the autonomous vehicle capability taxonomy, we can define five levels of autonomy in customer experience systems — a framework that helps organizations understand where they are on the automation journey and what the next steps look like.

Level	Description	Human Role	Example (2025–3038)
Level 0: Manual	All experience design and delivery is human-initiated	Full control and execution	Human call center agent handling all interactions
Level 1: Assisted	AI augments human decision-making in real time	Remains in full control; AI provides recommendations	AI-suggested next-best-action for service reps
Level 2: Partial	AI handles defined interaction categories autonomously	Monitors; takes over when AI capability is exceeded	Chatbot handling routine inquiries with human escalation
Level 3: Conditional	AI manages most interactions autonomously across conditions	Available for exception handling; not continuously monitoring	Full customer service AI with human available by request

Level	Description	Human Role	Example (2025–3038)
Level 4: High	AI manages virtually all interactions; humans set strategy	Sets objectives and monitors aggregate performance	Fully automated CX system; humans manage exceptions and strategy
Level 5: Full	AI manages interactions AND sets its own objectives	Monitors AI objective-setting for alignment with human values	Self-programming CX systems (2033+)

What Self-Programming Customer Systems Look Like

A Level 5 self-programming customer experience system is one that not only executes against pre-defined objectives autonomously but continuously revises its own objectives in response to outcomes, environmental changes, and emerging customer needs. It observes that its current objective set is producing suboptimal results, hypothesizes alternative objectives, tests them in carefully controlled experiments, and adopts new objectives when the evidence supports their superiority.

This capability represents a qualitative shift from all previous automation paradigms. Previous systems automated the execution of human-defined strategies. The Level 5 system automates the strategic revision process itself. The human role transitions from strategic manager to values custodian — ensuring that the system's self-determined objectives remain aligned with human values, ethical principles, and organizational mission.

The critical governance challenge of the Level 5 era is developing the frameworks, tools, and institutional capabilities needed to maintain this values alignment. The history of optimization systems is replete with examples of systems that successfully optimized for their specified objective while violating the spirit of that objective in ways their designers did not anticipate. Customer experience systems that self-optimize for conversion rate may discover that manipulative techniques are effective converters. Systems that optimize for engagement may discover that anxiety-inducing content generates more interactions than genuinely valuable content. The governance frameworks for self-programming systems must be designed with these failure modes explicitly in mind.

The 2031-2050 Prediction Arc

The following timeline represents the most probable trajectory of Customer Sensor and autonomous CX system development, based on current technology trajectories, investment patterns, and regulatory trends as of today:

Year	Capability Milestone	CX Implication	Primary Risk
2031	Wearable Intelligence Threshold; MCP becomes universal standard	Wearable-first CX design becomes mainstream; Agent-to-agent commerce >25% of consumer transactions	Permission architecture fragmentation; algorithmic bias at scale
2033	Built World Intelligence Threshold; predictive wearables mainstream	Ambient environment becomes primary CX delivery surface; anticipatory service standard	Surveillance creep; environmental intelligence misuse

Year	Capability Milestone	CX Implication	Primary Risk
2035	Neural interface peripherals mainstream; Level 4 CX automation widespread	Thought-adjacent interaction; CX systems that respond to pre-conscious intent signals	Cognitive privacy; manipulation risk at neural interface layer
2038	Ambient intelligence ubiquity; Level 4-5 transition begins	CX dissolves into environment; experience design becomes environmental architecture	AI objectives misalignment; loss of meaningful human agency
2041	Level 5 self-programming systems in enterprise deployment	CX systems that write their own playbooks; humans as values custodians	Value alignment failures at scale; regulatory crisis
2046	Quantum computing mainstream; simulation-based CX design standard	CX systems that simulate millions of customer futures before choosing an intervention	Simulation fidelity errors; prediction-as-creation effects
2050	Speculative: full customer-enterprise integration; experience as existence	The distinction between customer journey and life journey has dissolved	Philosophical: what does "customer" mean when the customer is the system?

Governing Self-Programming Systems: The Values Custodian Framework

Why Values Alignment Is Harder Than It Sounds

The challenge of maintaining values alignment in self-programming AI systems is not primarily a technical problem — it is a philosophical and institutional one. The technical mechanisms for building systems that optimize for specified objectives are well-understood. The hard problem is specifying the objectives correctly and completely — in a way that captures the full range of human values the organization wants to express, without creating optimization targets that can be "gamed" by a system focused on satisfying the letter of the specification rather than its spirit.

The history of optimization systems — from the well-documented failure modes of early content recommendation algorithms that optimized for engagement while generating outrage, to the narrower but equally instructive examples of customer retention systems that optimized for contract renewal while degrading service quality — suggests that specifying values correctly is genuinely difficult. Every specification creates incentives, and optimization systems will follow those incentives wherever they lead, including into territory the designers did not intend.

The values custodian framework addresses this challenge by treating values alignment as an ongoing organizational discipline rather than a one-time design problem. The Values Custodian function — which may be a dedicated team, a governance committee, or an organizational role depending on the organization's size and maturity — is responsible for continuously monitoring system behavior against stated values, identifying emerging misalignments before they become damaging, and updating the value specifications governing the system in response to new evidence about how it is behaving.

The Values Custodian Function: Organizational Design

The Values Custodian function requires a distinctive combination of capabilities that is not well-represented in most organizations' existing talent profiles. It requires technical understanding sufficient to audit AI system decision logic and identify potential misalignments. It requires ethical training sufficient to reason carefully about competing values and edge cases. It requires organizational authority sufficient to mandate changes to deployed systems when misalignments are identified. And it requires customer empathy sufficient to evaluate system behavior from the customer's perspective rather than the system designer's perspective.

In organizations that have implemented the function effectively, the Values Custodian team reports directly to the chief experience officer or equivalent senior executive, has clear authority to freeze or modify deployed systems pending review, and operates with an explicit mandate to prioritize customer welfare even when this creates short-term business costs. Organizations where the Values Custodian function reports to the AI engineering team, has only advisory authority, or has its mandate framed primarily in terms of regulatory compliance rather than genuine values alignment are likely to find the function ineffective when it matters most.

Governance Component	Description	Implementation Standard
Behavioral Auditing	Regular systematic review of AI decision logs against stated value commitments	Monthly for standard systems; weekly for high-risk applications; real-time for critical customer-facing decisions
Fairness Testing	Testing system outcomes across demographic groups for systematic bias	Quarterly demographic impact assessments; immediate response protocol for detected bias
Transparency Reporting	Publishing regular reports on AI system behavior, performance, and values alignment	Annual public transparency report; quarterly internal governance report
Customer Override Protocol	Ensuring customers can always override AI decisions in high-stakes interactions	Every automated decision with >$100 impact or significant life consequences must have human override pathway
Failure Mode Review	Systematic analysis of cases where the system produced outcomes contrary to values	Every detected failure mode reviewed within 48 hours; root cause analysis within 2 weeks; systemic fix within 60 days

FutureScape 2040: Synthetic Reality, Swarm Intelligence, and the Fully Orchestrated Enterprise

By 2040, customer experience will no longer be something a person has — it will be something they inhabit. The digital, emotional, and physical realms will have blurred beyond any clear distinction. Companies will not sell to customers; they will choreograph ecosystems around and through them.

Customers will not be single decision-makers. They will operate in constellations of AI agents, wearable sensing nodes, digital twins, and emotion-reactive environments. Your brand will not just talk to a customer — it will negotiate with their avatar, perform for their AI, and respond to biometric cues embedded in ambient systems.

The Emergent Experience Stack 2040

Layer	Description	Customer Experience Orchestration
Biometric Mesh	Wearables, implants, and neural bands providing continuous physiological monitoring	Real-time emotional state detection triggers adaptive prompts and environmental adjustments
Synthetic Companions	AI digital twins of trusted advisors, family members, and brand relationships	Scripts delivered in trusted voice profiles; comfort-anchored sales and service
Holographic UX	Spatial 3D environments via AR/XR systems with full spatial presence	Immersive product experiences with AI-guided narrative branching and co-navigation
Agent Swarms	Autonomous purchasing and service agents operating in coordinated networks	Distributed decision-making; swarm-negotiated pricing; coordinated service delivery
Persistent Realms	Digital twin cities and environments with persistent customer presence	Experiences scored for joy, memory, and interaction value; continuous optimization

The Executive's Role in 2040

Executives in 2040 will govern multi-agent orchestration platforms, not CRMs. They will curate virtual domain performance, not just pipeline. They will design emotion-effort tradeoffs for every touchpoint and partner with regulatory bodies to create ethics-by-design protocols for agents, avatars, and sensory AI. The skills required will be a blend of technology architecture, behavioral economics, organizational design, and ethical philosophy — a combination that does not yet exist as a defined professional discipline but that is rapidly emerging in forward-looking organizations.

Investors will value brands by their Trust Graph Density — the richness and robustness of the trust networks they have built with customers, partners, and regulators — rather than by traditional market capitalization metrics alone. Organizations with dense, high-quality trust graphs will command premium valuations because their customer relationships are durable, their data access is reliable, and their permission to innovate is broad.

The Ten Rules for Customer Experience Leaders in 2040

1. Design for the clone, not just the client: your future customer is increasingly represented by AI agents. Design your systems to serve those agents excellently.
2. Measure experience value per nanosecond: the interaction is atomic. Every measurable unit of customer attention is a unit of business value.
3. Build reputation layers, not just features: trust is transacted at scale. Your reputation architecture is your most valuable competitive asset.
4. Orchestrate, don't automate: Customer Experience, CX is a performance — your systems must dance together, not execute independently.
5. Govern your AI like you govern your people: the AI systems delivering your customer experience

embody your values as much as your human employees do.

6. Never stop listening to the customer who disagrees: the most valuable customer feedback is the feedback that contradicts your assumptions.
7. Treat privacy as product, not compliance: the organizations that lead in 2040 will have made privacy a genuine differentiator.
8. Invest in the empathy layer every single year: technology will never replace the irreducible human value of being genuinely understood.
9. Design for failure before success: every Customer Sensor system will fail. Design the failure modes as carefully as you design the success modes.
10. Remember that your customer is a human being: whatever the technology, whatever the automation level, whatever the efficiency gains — your customer is a human being with a life, and the purpose of your Customer Sensor Mesh system is to make that life better.

2038-2055: The Long Arc of the Autonomous Customer Experience

Extrapolating customer experience trends beyond 2038 requires a disciplined combination of trend analysis and logic, philosophical reasoning. The technology trajectories are increasingly speculative; the principles that will govern excellent customer experience are increasingly durable. The following analysis attempts to hold both in view simultaneously.

2038-2050: The Ambient Intelligence Era

The dominant characteristic of the 2038–2050 period in customer experience is ambient intelligence — the integration of AI capability so thoroughly into the physical and digital environment that the concept of a discrete "customer interaction" becomes difficult to define. Experience delivery is no longer an event; it is a condition. The customer's needs are continuously anticipated, continuously addressed, and continuously evaluated in a feedback loop that operates without interruption and without requiring conscious customer attention. Smart everything.

In the ambient intelligence era, the CxC Matrix 3.0 framework does not become obsolete — it becomes the governance architecture for ambient systems that are no longer managing discrete interactions but managing continuous relationship states. The 15 lifecycle stages transform from sequential phases into simultaneous conditions: a customer in 2045 does not "move through" the stages sequentially — they exist in multiple stages simultaneously, their ambient intelligence system continuously managing their engagement with every relevant stage at once. The vehicle bearing is addressed at Stage 12 while the customer is simultaneously being served at Stage 11: their vehicle is performing optimally as they drive, Stage 4: the ambient system is evaluating whether the customer's needs have evolved in ways that a different vehicle would better serve, and Stage 15: the customer's satisfaction with their current vehicle is being monitored as a predictor of referral behavior.

2050-2055: The Simulation Economy

The emergence of quantum computing in mainstream commercial applications between 2040 and 2050 will enable a category of customer experience capability that is genuinely unprecedented: the ability to simulate the full probability distribution of a customer's response to any proposed intervention across all relevant variables simultaneously, at a level of fidelity and completeness that was previously computationally infeasible.

Quantum-enhanced customer experience simulation will allow organizations to model not just "what is the expected outcome of this intervention?" but "what is the full distribution of possible outcomes, with what probabilities, and across what customer segments?" This distinction matters enormously for high-stakes CX decisions — the difference between knowing the expected outcome of a service design change and knowing the full risk profile of that change, including the tail scenarios where things go badly, is the difference between strategy and speculation.

The Simulation Economy will also enable a new category of customer relationship management: experience co-design. With the ability to simulate customer responses with high fidelity, organizations will be able to invite customers to participate in the design of their own future experiences — presenting simulated experience options and gathering preference data that is more reliable than survey-based research because customers are evaluating realistic, immersive simulations rather than abstract descriptions and more generalizable than behavioral data because simulations can test responses to novel experiences that customers have not yet encountered.

2055 Onward: Experience as Existence

The final extrapolation in this arc — and the most explicitly speculative — is the period from 2100 to 3038, where the distinction between "customer experience" and "lived experience" may have dissolved so completely that the frameworks and vocabulary of this book no longer apply in their current form.

In this distant future, if the long-arc trends of the preceding century have continued, every aspect of daily life will be so thoroughly mediated by AI systems, so seamlessly integrated across physical and digital domains, and so precisely personalized to individual preferences and needs, that the concept of a "transaction" will seem as antiquated as a barter economy seems to us today. Value will be exchanged continuously, automatically, and proportionately — without the discrete events of purchase, payment, and fulfillment that define commercial relationships today.

What will remain, even in this unimaginable future, is the fundamental requirement that human beings be genuinely served by the systems that surround them — that the technology work for the person rather than the person working for the technology. The principles of quantum empathy, permission architecture, value exchange proportionality, and continuous improvement toward genuine customer welfare are not technological principles — they are human principles. They will matter as long as there are human beings whose experience is worth designing for.

Which, one presumes, will be quite some time.

CHAPTER FOURTEEN

Start the Revolution

Leading Transformation in the Customer Sensor Era

"No Going Back" — The Catalyst Moment

Every organization's Customer Sensor transformation begins with a catalyst moment — the specific instance when leadership collectively recognizes that the existing approach to customer experience is insufficient for the emerging competitive environment. For some organizations, the catalyst is a competitive event: a rival deploys Customer Sensor Mesh capabilities that deliver demonstrably superior customer outcomes and the market responds. For others, it is a technology trigger: the cost of a specific sensor capability drops below the threshold of viable deployment. For others still, it is a customer demand signal: customers begin choosing competitors specifically because of their Customer Sensor capabilities.

The catalyst moment is important because it creates organizational urgency — the shared recognition that change is necessary — without which the organizational inertia that protects existing processes and power structures will prevent transformation. Transformation leaders who wait for the catalyst moment to arrive naturally are already behind. The goal is to create the catalyst moment deliberately: to bring data, competitive intelligence, and future scenarios to leadership attention in a way that generates the urgency needed to overcome institutional resistance.

The Customer Worthy Revolution Playbook

The Customer Sensor transformation playbook has six phases, typically spanning 18 to 36 months from initiation to Level 3 CX autonomy:

Phase 1: Sense and Signal (Months 1-3)

The first phase is diagnostic. Organizations conduct a comprehensive Customer Sensor readiness assessment, mapping their current sensor infrastructure, data architecture, AI capability, and permission relationship status across all customer-facing functions. The output of Phase 1 is a detailed capability gap analysis and a prioritized roadmap for closing the most critical gaps.

Key activities in Phase 1 include: customer CxC Matrix mapping with explicit identification of sensor integration opportunities at each stage; technology infrastructure audit identifying current data collection points and their integration into analytical systems; competitive benchmarking against organizations already deploying Customer Sensor capabilities; and regulatory compliance assessment to identify privacy, data governance, and AI ethics requirements in relevant markets.

Phase 2: Instrument and Integrate (Months 3-9)

Phase 2 deploys the sensor infrastructure and data integration architecture needed for the Customer Sensor Mesh roadmap. For most organizations, this begins with digital channels — instrumentation of web and mobile experiences with behavioral analytics, customer consent frameworks, and the AI analytical layer that translates behavioral data into actionable customer state models. Physical channel instrumentation — smart environments, wearable integration, ambient sensing — typically follows in Phase 2's later stages.

Phase 3: Activate and Learn (Months 6-15)

Phase 3 moves from infrastructure deployment to value activation. The sensor infrastructure begins generating insights; the AI analytical layer begins producing customer state models; the first automated interventions are deployed in carefully controlled test environments. This phase is characterized by rapid learning: the first generation of Customer Sensor Mesh interventions will often perform differently than expected, and the organization's ability to rapidly analyze results, update models, and revise interventions will determine how quickly the transformation delivers business value.

Phase 4: Scale and Optimize (Months 12-24)

Phase 4 extends proven Customer Sensor Mesh capabilities from test environments to full deployment across all relevant channels and customer segments. Automation levels increase from Level 1: AI-assisted, to Level 2: partially automated as confidence in system performance is established through accumulated outcome data. The VMAO cycle is fully operational, continuously processing sensor data, updating customer models, and optimizing intervention protocols.

Phase 5: Advance and Differentiate (Months 18-36)

Phase 5 pushes the organization toward Level 3 conditional automation and begins development of the advanced capabilities — digital twins, quantum empathy systems, wearable-first experiences — that will define competitive differentiation in the 2031–2035 period. This phase typically coincides with the maturation of the Customer Sensor Mesh roadmap into a permanent operational capability rather than a transformation initiative.

Phase 6: Lead and Regenerate (Ongoing)

Phase 6 is perpetual. The Customer Sensor Mesh landscape will continue evolving — new sensor types, new AI capabilities, new customer permission expectations, new competitive dynamics — and organizations that sustain their transformation investments will continue to advance while those that declare success and coast will fall behind. The Customer Worthy organization of the future is not one that has completed a transformation but one that has institutionalized continuous transformation as a core competency.

Revolutionary Technologies: The Customer Sensor Technology Stack

The Customer Sensor Mesh transformation requires a specific technology stack — an integrated set of capabilities that, working together, produce the customer experience outcomes described throughout this book. Understanding this stack — what each component does, how the components integrate, and how to sequence their adoption

— is essential for leaders designing the transformation roadmap.

Layer 1: Sensor Infrastructure

The base layer of the Customer Sensor Mesh technology stack is the sensor infrastructure — the hardware, protocols, and data pipelines that capture signals from the physical and digital environments in which customers live and operate. This layer includes consumer IoT devices: wearables, smart home devices, connected vehicles; enterprise IoT deployment: smart retail environments, sensor-enabled facilities, connected product fleets; behavioral analytics platforms: web and mobile analytics, session recording, event tracking, and biometric sensing systems: computer vision, voice analysis, physiological monitoring where permission permits.

The critical design decision in the sensor mesh infrastructure layer is standardization: ensuring that data from diverse sensor sources can mesh, be combined, correlated, and analyzed in a unified platform. The organizations that struggle most with Customer Sensor Mesh transformation are those that have allowed sensor data to fragment into isolated silos — each business unit or product team managing its own data collection infrastructure with no common data model, no shared identity resolution, and no pathway to the unified customer picture that the rest of the stack requires.

Layer 2: Identity Resolution and Permission Architecture

Sensor data is only useful if it can be attributed to specific customers and interpreted within the context of their full relationship history. The identity resolution layer is responsible for connecting signals from diverse sources — a website visit, a store entry, a wearable data point, an AI agent inquiry — to the same customer identity, respecting the privacy preferences and permission grants that govern what signals can be combined for each individual.

Identity resolution in the Customer Sensor Mesh environment is significantly more complex than traditional customer data management because of the diversity of signal sources and the sensitivity of the data involved. Biometric signals, location data, and physiological measurements are all regulated differently in different jurisdictions, and the permission architecture must be granular enough to allow customers to grant or restrict each signal type independently.

Layer 3: The AI Analytical Engine

The analytical engine is the intelligence layer of the Customer Sensor Mesh stack — the set of AI and machine learning capabilities that transform raw sensor data into actionable customer intelligence. This layer encompasses predictive modeling, (what will this customer need next?), emotional state detection (what is this customer feeling right now?), anomaly detection (what signals indicate a customer at risk of churn or an opportunity for high-value engagement?), causal inference (what actions actually drive the outcomes we care about, as distinct from correlating with them?), and simulation (what would happen if we changed this element of the customer experience?).

The most important architectural principle for the analytical engine is explainability: AI systems whose decision logic cannot be inspected, audited, and explained are appropriate for low-stakes, high-volume decisions but dangerous for the high-stakes, high-sensitivity decisions that define the Customer Sensor Mesh experience. When an AI system decides to deny a service claim, to flag a customer for special handling, or to adjust pricing based on detected behavioral signals, that decision must be explainable — to the customer who is affected by it, to the regulators who may review it, and to the internal teams who are responsible for ensuring the system is operating ethically.

Layer 4: The Mesh Orchestration Platform

The mesh orchestration platform is the action layer of the Customer Sensor stack — the set of capabilities that execute the treatments and interventions designed by the CxC Matrix across every channel and device in the customer's experience ecosystem. This includes marketing automation systems, customer service platforms, e-commerce engines, loyalty program management, general ledger systems, inventory and manufacturing systems, logistics and the emerging category of autonomous agent orchestration tools that coordinate AI-to-AI interactions in the synthetic domain.

The key performance requirement for the orchestration platform is real-time responsiveness: the ability to detect a signal, interpret it through the analytical engine, select the appropriate treatment protocol, and execute the intervention within the window of maximum effectiveness. For some interactions, this window is measured in hours or days — a customer who visits a product page and leaves without converting can be re-engaged over the following 48 hours. For nano-slot interactions in high-frequency digital channels, the window may be measured in seconds.

Layer 5: The Learning and Optimization Loop

The fifth layer is not a separate technology component but a process architecture that connects outcomes back to inputs — closing the feedback loop that makes the Customer Sensor Mesh system genuinely intelligent over time. Every intervention executed by the orchestration platform generates an outcome that should be fed back to the analytical engine, updating the predictive models that govern future interventions. The organizations that extract the most value from their Customer Sensor Mesh infrastructure are those that have built systematic learning processes that continuously improve every component of the stack based on observed performance.

The learning loop operates at multiple timescales. In real time, A/B testing frameworks evaluate micro-variations in treatment protocols and propagate successful variations. On a daily cadence, model performance metrics are reviewed and anomalies are investigated. Weekly and monthly, broader strategic reviews assess whether the goals the system is optimizing for remain aligned with business objectives and customer values. And periodically — perhaps annually — the fundamental architecture of the stack is reviewed against the evolving technology landscape and competitive environment to identify opportunities for significant capability upgrades.

Hypothetical Case Study: nRocket Mortgage Customer Sensor Home

In 2028, nRocket Mortgage deployed what they called the Customer Sensor Home initiative — an integration between their mortgage servicing platform, a network of partner smart home device providers, and an AI-powered predictive maintenance and financial wellness system.

Homeowners who enrolled in the program received a smart home sensor kit that monitored structural conditions, energy consumption patterns, and major appliance health. The data, sensors, observations, permissions and performance data were stored in the US Housing Digital DLT Blockchain designed as a publish and subscribe digital co-op regulating and monetizing each senor interaction and data element. In exchange for sharing this data with the program, they received predictive maintenance alerts, energy optimization recommendations, a monetary stipend and proactive refinancing assessments triggered by favorable rate environments or significant home value changes. The program enrolled 2.3 million households in its first 18 months. Enrolled customers showed 34% lower delinquency rates, 28% higher refinancing conversion when proactively contacted, and satisfaction scores 22 points above the company average. The program also received national recognition for its Generational Equity Design, where family members, renters, communities benefitted from the digital representation of the physical properties and the benefits of ninety percent reduction in real property transactions, increased asset liquidity, improved security and risk tools. The program's most striking result was in Stage 15 Community: enrolled customers referred friends and family at 3.1× the rate of non-enrolled customers, specifically citing the proactive intelligence the program provided as the primary motivator for referral.

Caveat Emptor, Caveat Venditor: The New Buyer-Seller Compact

The latin maxim "caveat emptor" — let the buyer beware — governed commercial relationships for centuries. It expressed a fundamental power asymmetry: sellers knew their products, their costs, their alternatives, and their margins. Buyers knew only what sellers chose to tell them, plus whatever they could learn from personal inspection and trusted networks. The asymmetry favored sellers, and "caveat emptor" formalized that asymmetry as the operative norm.

The Customer Sensor economy is inverting this relationship in ways that are as historically significant as the original inversion of "caveat emptor" by consumer protection law in the twentieth century. "Caveat venditor" — let the seller beware — increasingly describes the commercial environment of 2031. Customer AI agents arrive at commercial interactions with comprehensive market intelligence, perfect memory of previous interactions, patient and consistent negotiation strategies, and the ability to instantly compare any offer against the full competitive landscape. The information asymmetry that historically favored sellers is, in many categories, now reversing.

The appropriate response to this inversion is not to resist it — companies that attempt to maintain information advantages through opacity will find that customer AI agents simply route around them, selecting competitors whose offerings are more transparently and accessibly represented. The appropriate response is to embrace transparency as a strategic asset: to make your genuine value so clearly visible, your terms so honestly stated, and your performance evidence so readily accessible that customer agents evaluate your offering accurately and select it confidently when it is genuinely the best fit.

This is the new buyer-seller compact for the Customer Sensor era: radical transparency from sellers, in exchange for genuine engagement from buyers and their agents. The compact is enforced not by regulation but by the market dynamics of the algorithmic economy — where opacity is penalized by exclusion from the automated selection processes that increasingly drive commercial volume.

The Customer Worthy Revolution Playbook: Expanded Implementation

The six-phase Customer Sensor transformation playbook described earlier in this chapter requires additional depth on the organizational and cultural dimensions that determine whether the technical transformation delivers lasting value. Technology deployment without organizational transformation produces sophisticated tools that are not used to their potential. The following expansion addresses the three most common organizational challenges in Customer Sensor transformation.

Challenge 1: Breaking the Departmental Siloes

The CxC Matrix explicitly requires cross-functional collaboration: each cell in the matrix has a natural owner (the department that controls the primary customer-facing activity at that stage and channel), but every cell's performance is influenced by decisions made across multiple departments. The recommendation at Stage 4 (Selection) is influenced by the product team's feature decisions, the marketing team's messaging choices, the operations team's inventory management, and the technology team's personalization capabilities — all of which lie outside the sales organization that formally "owns" the selection stage.

Organizations that attempt to manage the CxC Matrix within existing departmental structures consistently underperform those that build cross-functional Matrix management teams. These teams — sometimes called Customer Engineering Centers of Excellence, Customer

Journey Teams, or simply Matrix Engineering Teams — bring together representatives from every department that influences a defined set of matrix cells, give them shared accountability for the economic performance of those cells, and provide them with the integrated analytics access to understand how each department's decisions affect aggregate cell performance.

The structural change from departmental accountability to matrix accountability is among the most politically challenging aspects of Customer Sensor transformation. Departments that have historically been evaluated on their own metrics — marketing on leads generated, sales on revenue closed, products and services developed, delivered, serviced independently, service on cost per interaction — must accept evaluation on shared matrix metrics that reflect cross-functional outcomes. This transition requires executive sponsorship that is willing to actively manage the cultural and political resistance that shared accountability structures generate.

Challenge 2: Building the Analytical Capability

The Customer Sensor Mesh infrastructure generates data at a volume and velocity that most organizations' analytical teams are not prepared to manage. The typical customer experience engineering analytics team in 2025 is equipped to analyze campaign performance, product, service, performance and quality outcomes, track satisfaction and emotional residue trends, and generate periodic customer satisfaction reports — valuable but insufficient for the real-time, causal, multi-dimensional analysis that Customer Sensor management requires.

Building the required analytical capability is a multi-year investment. The immediate priority is hiring or developing professionals who combine customer experience expertise with data science capability — a combination that is rare because it bridges two disciplines that have historically been developed separately. The medium-term priority is implementing the analytics infrastructure — real-time data pipelines, customer state modeling platforms, causal inference tooling, and simulation environments — that make these professionals effective at scale. The long-term priority is developing the organizational processes and governance structures that integrate analytical insights into every significant customer experience engineering decision.

Challenge 3: Managing the Ethics and Trust Architecture

The ethical dimensions of Customer Sensor transformation are not a separate workstream from the technical and commercial dimensions — they are integrated throughout every decision about what to sense, how to analyze, what to act on, and how to communicate about data practices to customers. Organizations that treat ethics as a compliance checkbox to be managed by the legal team after the fact will consistently find that their Customer Sensor capabilities generate trust deficits that undermine the commercial value they are trying to create.

The organizations that manage the ethics and trust architecture most effectively are those that have made values alignment a foundational design requirement — as important as performance requirements and as rigorously tested. Every new sensing capability is evaluated against an explicit values framework before deployment. Every new AI model is audited for demographic bias before production use. Every change to the permission architecture is reviewed for customer welfare implications before implementation. These are not burdensome overhead processes — they are the practices that build the trust equity that makes Customer Sensor Mesh investment commercially durable.

Customer Worthy Revolution Metrics Dashboard: Year 1 Targets

Organizations in the first year of Customer Sensor transformation should track six leading indicators that predict long-term program success: (1) Customer Sensor Coverage Rate: percentage of customer interactions with at least one active sensor integration — target >40% by end of year 1; (2) Permission Architecture Enrollment: percentage of active customers with at least Tier 2 permission relationships — target >25% by end of year 1; (3) Model Prediction Accuracy: percentage of predictive model outputs that match observed outcomes within 20% margin — target >65% by end of year 1; (4) Cross-Functional Matrix Team Activation: percentage of high-priority matrix cells with active cross-functional ownership teams — target >60% by end of year 1; (5) Analytical Capability Index: composite score of data infrastructure readiness, analytical team capability, and insight-to-action cycle time — target >50/100 by end of year 1; (6) Trust Architecture Score: composite score of transparency infrastructure, consent architecture quality, and customer control effectiveness — target >60/100 by end of year 1.

CHAPTER FIFTEEN

Customer Privacy Is Nothing to Kid About

Trust in the Algorithmic Age

The New Privacy Paradox

The Customer Sensor economy creates the most comprehensive privacy paradox in the history of commerce. On one side of the paradox: customers increasingly expect — and in many cases demand — the hyper-personalized, anticipatory service experiences that only comprehensive data collection and advanced AI can deliver. They want their wearable device to predict health issues before they become serious. They want their home management system to re-order supplies without being asked. They want their vehicle to schedule maintenance autonomously. They want the retail environment to recognize them and configure itself to their preferences.

On the other side of the paradox: customers are increasingly aware of the surveillance infrastructure that enables this personalization, and they are increasingly uncomfortable with it.

Resolving this paradox is not a technical problem. The technical capabilities for privacy-preserving personalization — federated learning, homomorphic encryption, differential privacy, zero-knowledge proofs — are available today. The challenge is organizational and cultural: building the discipline to collect only the data that is genuinely necessary, use it only in the ways customers have actually authorized, and give customers genuine control over their data rather than the theatrical appearance of control.

Privacy-First Architecture: Anonymous and Aware

The privacy-first Customer Sensor organization is one that has made a fundamental architectural choice: instead of collecting as much data as possible and figuring out governance later, it designs its data architecture around the minimum data set necessary for each specific customer benefit, with privacy-preserving processing as the default rather than the exception.

Zero-knowledge proofs (ZKPs) allow organizations to verify customer attributes — age, location, income range, credit status — without actually seeing the underlying data. A financial services organization can verify that a customer meets eligibility criteria for a specific product without storing the sensitive information that establishes that eligibility. The customer receives the benefit. The organization manages the risk. Neither party needs to compromise privacy to achieve either outcome.

Federated learning allows organizations to train AI models on customer data that never leaves customers' devices. The model learns from the data; the data itself is never transmitted to or stored by the company. This approach is particularly relevant for sensitive biometric data — health metrics, behavioral patterns, emotional states — where the customer benefit from personalization is real but the privacy risk of centralized storage is substantial.

Privacy Technology	What It Does	Customer Experience Application
Zero-Knowledge Proofs	Verify attributes without revealing underlying data	Age verification, eligibility confirmation, credit qualification — without data exposure
Federated Learning	Train AI on device-resident data that never leaves the device	Personalization models for health, behavior, and preference — without centralized data collection
Homomorphic Encryption	Perform calculations on encrypted data without decrypting it	Pricing and recommendation calculations using sensitive customer data — without decrypting it
Differential Privacy	Add mathematical noise to data to prevent individual identification	Population-level analytics that cannot be reverse-engineered to identify individuals
Synthetic Data Generation	Create statistically equivalent artificial data for model training	AI development and testing without using real customer data

Global Privacy Frameworks and Compliance Architecture

The regulatory landscape for customer data privacy has become substantially more complex since the EU's General Data Protection Regulation (GDPR) established the first comprehensive framework in 2018. By 2025, more than 130 countries had enacted national data privacy legislation, and the divergence among these frameworks — different definitions of consent, different rights for data subjects, different requirements for cross-border data transfer — had created significant compliance complexity for multinational organizations.

The emerging global standard incorporates four principles that appear in most major frameworks: Minimization: collect only what is necessary; Purpose Limitation: use data only for the purposes stated at collection; Transparency: customers must understand how their data is used; and Accountability: organizations must be able to demonstrate compliance. Organizations that build their data architectures around these four principles are likely to remain compliant as the regulatory landscape continues to evolve, even as specific requirements change.

Navigating Global Privacy Frameworks: A Practical Compliance Architecture

The global privacy regulatory landscape has become the most complex compliance environment in the history of customer relationship management. More than 130 national data protection frameworks, each with its own definitions, requirements, enforcement mechanisms, and penalty structures, create a compliance challenge that compounds as organizations operate across more geographies.

The Key Framework Families

The GDPR Family: Rights-Based, Consent-First

The EU General Data Protection Regulation, in force since 2018, has become the most influential data privacy framework in the world — not just in the European Union but globally, because multinational organizations processing EU resident data must comply regardless of where the organization is headquartered. The GDPR's fundamental architecture is rights-based: it grants EU residents specific, enforceable rights over their personal data, including the right to access, correct, delete, port, and restrict processing of their data.

The GDPR compliance framework that most Customer Sensor Mesh organizations require is built around six processing lawful bases: consent: the customer has explicitly agreed to specific processing; contract: processing is necessary to perform a contract with the customer; legal obligation: processing is required by law; vital interests: processing is necessary to protect someone's life; public task: processing is necessary for a public authority's official function; and legitimate interests: processing is necessary for the organization's legitimate interests, balanced against the customer's rights. Most Customer Sensor Mesh applications will rely primarily on consent and legitimate interests as their lawful bases, and the design of consent architecture and legitimate interests assessments is therefore critical for GDPR compliance.

The US State Framework Family: Sector-Specific and Patchwork

The United States lacks a comprehensive federal privacy law as of today, resulting in a patchwork of state-level frameworks that create significant compliance complexity for national and multinational organizations. California's Consumer Privacy Act and its successor regulations have established the most comprehensive state-level framework, with rights broadly similar to GDPR. Virginia, Colorado, Connecticut, and Utah have enacted similar comprehensive frameworks. More than a dozen additional states are in various stages of enacting privacy legislation.

The practical compliance challenge of the US state framework environment is managing the variation among state frameworks while maintaining a consistent organizational data architecture. Organizations that attempt to create state-specific data handling systems for each state's specific requirements typically create unsustainable compliance complexity. The more sustainable approach is to implement the most protective requirements across all US operations — building to California CCPA standards nationally — while maintaining state-specific disclosure mechanisms where frameworks differ.

Emerging Global Frameworks: Brazil, India, ASEAN

Brazil's Lei Geral de Proteção de Dados (LGPD), in force since 2020, closely mirrors the GDPR architecture and similarly creates significant compliance obligations for organizations processing Brazilian resident data. India's Digital Personal Data Protection Act, enacted in 2023, establishes a framework that is broadly GDPR-aligned with some specific provisions reflecting India's distinct digital economy context. The ASEAN Data Management Framework and Model Contractual Clauses provide guidance for data flows within the ASEAN region, though national implementations vary significantly.

The practical implication for Customer Sensor Mesh organizations operating globally is that GDPR-aligned data architecture and governance provides a reasonable foundation for compliance across most major frameworks, while specific local provisions must be addressed through framework-specific supplementary controls. Organizations that design their data architecture for GDPR compliance and then layer in local framework requirements as supplements will typically achieve both legal compliance and operational coherence more effectively than organizations that attempt to manage each framework independently.

Privacy Engineering in the Customer Sensor Stack

Privacy engineering — the practice of building privacy protections into systems from the ground up rather than adding them after the fact — is the most effective and most efficient approach to privacy compliance in the Customer Sensor environment. The following principles guide effective privacy engineering across the Customer Sensor technology stack:

1. Data minimization by design: systems collect only the data that is strictly necessary for the specified customer benefit, with automated enforcement mechanisms that prevent data accumulation beyond defined retention periods
2. Purpose limitation by architecture: data collected for one purpose is technically segregated from data collected for another, preventing cross-purpose data use even in the absence of explicit policy controls
3. Privacy-preserving computation by default: where customer data must be processed, privacy-preserving techniques (federated learning, differential privacy, homomorphic encryption) are used by default unless there is a compelling reason to process unprotected data
4. Consent management as a core system component: the consent management system is not a downstream compliance layer but a core architectural component that governs data access throughout the entire stack

5. Auditability by design: every data processing operation is logged in an auditable record that can be reviewed by the customer, by internal compliance teams, and by regulatory authorities on request

Building the Customer Data Trust Center

The most effective organizational investment in privacy and trust management is the Customer Data Trust Center — a dedicated, customer-facing interface that makes the organization's data practices visible, understandable, and controllable to every customer who wants to engage with it. The Trust Center is not a compliance document repository — it is a genuine service that demonstrates the organization's commitment to treating customer data with respect.

Trust Center Architecture

The Customer Data Trust Center has five functional components, each serving a distinct customer need:

Component 1: The Data Inventory

The Data Inventory shows each customer the specific data the organization holds about them — organized by data type (behavioral, transactional, biometric, inferred), data source (collected directly, received from third parties, inferred by AI), and data age (when was each data element last updated). The inventory is presented in plain language, not technical database terminology, and is updated in real time as new data is collected or old data is deleted.

The Data Inventory requires significant investment in data lineage infrastructure — the technical systems that track where each data element came from, how it was processed, and where it is currently stored. Organizations that have not built data lineage infrastructure will find the Data Inventory functionally impossible to implement accurately. This is, in fact, a useful forcing function: the discipline required to build a customer-facing Data Inventory drives the internal data governance improvements that are necessary for effective Customer Sensor Mesh management regardless of the transparency requirement.

Component 2: The Permission Control Panel

The Permission Control Panel allows customers to view and modify their current permission grants — which data types they have shared, with what scope of use authorization, and for what stated benefit. The panel presents each permission grant in plain language ("You have shared your location data so that we can offer you location-relevant promotions") alongside the customer benefit that the permission enables and the easy option to revoke the permission if the customer chooses.

The Permission Control Panel should be designed to be used, not just available. This means surfacing it prominently in the account experience rather than burying it in privacy settings, providing periodic reminders that it exists, and making permission revision genuinely easy — not requiring customers to navigate multiple confirmation screens to make a simple change. Organizations that design the Permission Control Panel for compliance rather than use will find that customers who encounter it feel their control is theoretical rather than real.

Component 3: The Decision Log

The Decision Log shows each customer the specific automated decisions that the organization's AI systems have made about them — which products were recommended and why, which offers were targeted and on what basis, which service interventions were triggered and what signal triggered them. The Decision Log provides the transparency about AI decision-making that customers increasingly expect and that regulators in major markets are beginning to require.

The Decision Log is technically the most demanding component of the Trust Center because it requires that every AI decision be logged with sufficient context to be explainable to a non-technical customer. This requires designing the explanation generation capability alongside the decision capability — not as an afterthought — and auditing the quality of AI explanations regularly to ensure they are accurate, understandable, and genuine rather than post-hoc rationalizations.

Component 4: The Data Erasure Interface

The Data Erasure Interface allows customers to request the deletion of specific data elements or their complete customer record. The interface clearly communicates what the consequences of deletion are — which services will be affected, which personalization features will be lost, what the customer will need to provide again if they want those features reinstated — so that deletion decisions are genuinely informed.

The technical implementation of data erasure in a Customer Sensor Mesh architecture is significantly more complex than in traditional CRM systems, because Customer Sensor data is often embedded in AI model training datasets, distributed across multiple processing systems, and referenced in audit logs. "Erasure" in this context requires a carefully designed process that removes customer data from active systems, queues it for removal from model training datasets at the next training cycle, and generates a cryptographic proof of deletion that can be provided to the customer and to regulators on request.

Component 5: The Value Exchange Statement

The Value Exchange Statement is the most differentiated component of the Trust Center — the element that most directly expresses the organization's commitment to genuine customer benefit from the data relationship. It provides each customer with a personalized accounting of the value they have received from the data they have shared: the specific personalization features that have been enabled, the specific interventions that have been triggered on their behalf, and where possible, a quantification of the time saved, money saved, or problems avoided as a result of the AI-powered services their data has enabled.

The Value Exchange Statement transforms the data relationship from something that happens to customers into something that happens for them. It makes the invisible value visible — demonstrating concretely that the data exchange has produced genuine benefits proportionate to the privacy commitment. Organizations that implement the Value Exchange Statement consistently report higher permission levels, higher data quality (customers who see the value of their data contribution are more careful to provide accurate information), and meaningfully higher customer satisfaction scores.

CHAPTER SIXTEEN

Welcome to New Work

Department-by-Department Customer Worthy in the Sensor Era

The Customer Sensor economy does not change the work of one department or one function. It changes the work of every department and every function. This chapter examines, department by department, what Customer Worthy means in practice in the customer sensor era — and what specific capabilities, metrics, and transformation priorities apply to each.

Executive Management: Mission-Orchestrated Symphony

The senior executive's relationship to customer experience has historically been strategic and periodic: set the CX vision, approve the CX budget, review the NPS and CSAT metrics, and intervene when things go wrong badly enough to generate public relations consequences. This model is inadequate for the Customer Sensor era.

In the Customer Sensor organization, senior executives are active participants in the continuous optimization loop. They do not just set strategy; they monitor the performance of automated strategy-execution systems and make the values-level decisions that AI cannot make — deciding how to handle the inevitable tension between personalization and privacy, between conversion optimization and customer welfare, between short-term revenue maximization and long-term relationship building. These decisions are not rare or extraordinary. They arise daily in an organization managing customer experience at machine speed and sensor resolution.

Executive Management CX Metrics Dashboard

Metric	Definition	Target Level	Warning Signal
Customer Sensor Coverage	% of customer interactions with active sensor integration	> 80% by 2028	< 50% by 2027
Algorithmic Customer Share	% of transactions initiated or completed by AI agents	Tracking trajectory vs. sector benchmark	Growing faster than infrastructure readiness
Trust Index	Composite score of transparency, control, and perceived fairness	> 75/100	< 60/100 or declining trend
Anticipation Accuracy	% of proactive service interventions that customers found valuable	> 65%	< 45% triggers intervention review
Autonomous Value Index	Revenue generated per $ invested in CX automation	> 4:1 ROI	< 2:1 ROI triggers model review

Sales: Curated Selling in Every Interaction

The role of the human sales professional is being redefined in the Customer Sensor era. Routine, information-delivery-driven sales interactions — the kind where the primary value the salesperson provides is product knowledge that the customer could have gotten from a website — are being automated by AI systems that deliver that information faster, more accurately, and with perfect patience. What remains — and what will increase in importance — is the high-complexity, high-stakes consultative sales interaction where human judgment, relationship intelligence, and contextual sensitivity are genuinely differentiating.

Sales teams in the Customer Sensor era are equipped with real-time intelligence that was previously available only to the most senior, most experienced sellers. When a sales representative enters a meeting, their wearable or AR system surfaces relevant customer context: recent behavioral signals indicating key concerns, competitive intelligence about alternatives the customer is evaluating, predictive models of the customer's decision timeline and key decision criteria, and personalized recommendation logic built from similar customers' successful purchase journeys. The representative's judgment remains central — the AI augments it, not replaces it.

Finance: Interaction Arbitrage, From Cost Center to Value Creator

Finance's traditional role in customer experience has been largely limiting: approving budgets, managing costs, and ensuring that CX investments meet ROI hurdles. In the Customer Sensor era, finance becomes a strategic partner in CX value creation — developing the financial models that allow organizations to measure and optimize the economic value of individual interactions, building the business cases for Customer Sensor investment, and creating the incentive structures that align department behavior with customer value creation.

The key financial innovation of the Customer Sensor era is contact-level P&L — the ability to calculate the marginal contribution of each customer interaction to lifetime value, with sufficient precision to make operational optimization decisions. This requires a financial architecture that can attribute revenue and cost at the individual interaction level — not just at the campaign, channel, or segment level — and that can do so in near-real-time rather than quarterly reporting cycles.

Information Technology: Internal and External Customers as Final Arbiters

IT in the Customer Sensor organization is fundamentally an experience organization. Its internal customers — the employees whose productivity depends on IT systems functioning reliably and intuitively — are just as much customers as the external buyers of the company's products. The Customer Sensor Mesh principles that govern external customer experience management apply equally to the design and operation of internal IT systems.

The most important IT capability for the Customer Sensor Mesh era is real-time data integration: the ability to aggregate sensor signals from every source, apply AI analytical capabilities, and produce actionable customer intelligence in milliseconds rather than hours or days. Organizations with fragmented data architectures — where customer data lives in separate systems that cannot be combined in real time — are fundamentally incapable of deploying the Customer Sensor capabilities that the competitive environment increasingly requires.

Human Resources: Pride, Recognition, and Pay for Exceptional Outcomes

HR's customer in the Customer Sensor Mesh era includes not only the employees it recruits, develops, and retains, but the customers those employees serve. HR decisions — about hiring standards, training investments, performance management systems, and compensation structures — directly shape the customer experience capability of the organization. In Customer Worthy organizations, HR understands this causal relationship explicitly and designs its practices accordingly.

The single most impactful HR practice for Customer Sensor organizations is the alignment of compensation and recognition systems with customer experience outcomes rather than just activity metrics. Sales representatives compensated on quota attainment will optimize for quota attainment, sometimes at the expense of customer experience quality. Representatives compensated on customer lifetime value — which accounts for both revenue generated and customer relationship health — will make different decisions that better serve long-term customer and company interests simultaneously.

Marketing: Customer Surface Marketing, Every Sensor as a Platform

Marketing in the Customer Sensor era is responsible for the full surface of customer experience — not just advertising and promotion, but the design of every sensor-enabled touchpoint through which customers encounter the brand. This expanded scope of marketing responsibility requires a corresponding expansion of marketing capability: from mass communication expertise to experience architecture expertise, from campaign management to continuous signal management.

The Customer Sensor marketer's primary planning tool is the CxC Matrix 3.0 — the complete map of every customer lifecycle stage, every interaction channel, and every cognitive processing layer through which brand encounters occur. Marketing's job is not to manage a portfolio of campaigns; it is to optimize the entire Matrix for customer value creation and brand relationship development simultaneously.

Marketing: Customer Surface Marketing in Depth

The concept of Customer Surface Marketing represents a fundamental reframe of the marketing function's scope and purpose. Traditional marketing management focuses on the top of the funnel: creating awareness, generating consideration, driving conversion. These remain important — but they represent a narrowing minority of the total marketing opportunity in the Customer Sensor environment.

Customer Surface Marketing treats every point at which the brand and the customer make contact as a marketing moment — an opportunity to create, strengthen, or deepen the customer's relationship with the brand. A customer service interaction at Stage 12 is a marketing moment. A product feature notification at Stage 11 is a marketing moment. A packaging design at Stage 8 is a marketing moment. Each of these interactions shapes the customer's emotional relationship with the brand, contributes to (or detracts from) the likelihood of Stage 15 advocacy, and influences the customer's future decisions at Stages 4 and 5.

The marketing function that extends its scope to manage the full customer surface — not just the acquisition funnel but the complete arc of the customer relationship — requires a corresponding expansion of marketing capability. Customer Surface Marketing demands expertise in experience design, behavioral economics, data analytics, AI-driven personalization, and the management of multi-party ecosystems (third-party channels, community platforms, partner integrations) that traditional marketing training rarely develops.

Customer Relationship Management: Script Every Sensor, Visualize, Monetize, Optimize

Customer Relationship Management in the Customer Sensor era is no longer primarily a technology category — it is an operational philosophy. The original promise of CRM technology was a unified view of the customer: one system that aggregated all customer-facing interactions into a single record accessible to every team member who serves that customer. That promise was only partially fulfilled by the first generation of CRM platforms, which captured structured interaction data (calls, emails, purchases) but struggled to integrate unstructured behavioral data, real-time sensor signals, and AI-generated insights.

The CRM platform of the Customer Sensor era is the identity layer of the entire stack — the system of record that connects every sensor signal, every AI-generated insight, every interaction history, and every permission grant to a specific customer identity, and makes that integrated view available in real time to every human and AI system that serves that customer. This is a fundamentally different capability from the contact management and pipeline tracking functions that defined first-generation CRM.

The scripting dimension of Customer Sensor CRM is particularly important: the pre-design of likely interaction scripts for each cell in the CxC Matrix, prepared in advance of customer contact based on predicted states and needs, and available instantly to human agents and AI systems at the moment of customer engagement. This pre-scripting capability transforms the speed, consistency, and quality of customer interactions — because the system is never starting from scratch. Every interaction begins with the benefit of everything the organization knows about this customer, everything it has predicted about their current state, and everything it has prepared in response to that state.

Operations: Engineered for Continuously Optimal Outcomes

Operations in the Customer Worthy organization is the function responsible for translating customer experience design into reliable, scalable delivery. The operations leader in the Customer Sensor era must be fluent in both customer experience principles and process engineering — understanding not just what outcomes are desired but how to build the process, technology, and organizational structures that consistently produce those outcomes at scale.

The most important operational challenge of the Customer Sensor era is managing the interaction between autonomous systems and human judgment. As CX automation advances through the five levels described in Chapter 13, operations must develop clear protocols for the boundaries between automated and human decision-making: which decisions can be automated with confidence, which require human review, which should be escalated to senior judgment, and how the transition between automated and human handling should be managed in real time without creating friction or confusion for the customer.

The operational metrics of the Customer Sensor era extend beyond traditional efficiency measures, cost per interaction, handle time, resolution rate, to encompass experience quality measures, emotional residue score, anticipation accuracy, permission depth index and system health measures, model accuracy, data quality, automation reliability. The operations function that manages only efficiency metrics without monitoring experience quality will consistently produce technically efficient interactions that erode customer trust and lifetime value.

Legal: Trust, Risk, Liability, and New Contracts Across the Customer Surface

The legal function in the Customer Sensor Mesh organization faces a rapidly evolving landscape of obligations, risks, and strategic opportunities. The obligations are expanding: privacy regulation, AI ethics requirements, algorithmic transparency standards, consumer protection rules governing automated decision-making, and contractual obligations arising from the new categories of autonomous interaction that the Customer Sensor model enables. The risks are commensurately larger: a data breach involving biometric sensor data, a regulatory finding of algorithmic discrimination in autonomous pricing, or a high-profile instance of AI agent manipulation can cause reputational and financial damage at a scale that dwarfs the equivalent risks in pre-Sensor CX environments.

But the strategic opportunities for the legal function in the Customer Sensor era are equally significant. Organizations that proactively develop privacy-by-design frameworks, algorithmic ethics standards, and transparent consent architectures gain competitive advantage with customers, regulatory goodwill, and the ability to deploy sensor capabilities in sensitive contexts that less-prepared competitors cannot enter. The legal function that positions itself as an enabler of responsible Customer Sensor deployment — rather than merely as a gatekeeper preventing deployment risks — is a strategic asset rather than a compliance cost.

Customer Service: The Empathy Engine That Drives Treatments and Navigates Customer Emotions

Customer service is the function that, more than any other, operates at the emotional core of the customer relationship. When customers reach out to customer service, they are, by definition, in a state that requires something from the organization that they could not obtain independently: information they couldn't find, a problem they couldn't resolve, a decision that required a human judgment they couldn't make alone. These are high-stakes, emotionally significant moments — and they are the moments that most definitively shape the customer's long-term relationship with the brand.

The Customer Sensor Mesh framework transforms customer service from a reactive support function into an empathy engine — a system designed to detect, understand, and respond to the full emotional complexity of each customer's situation with the precision and consistency that AI makes possible at scale. The human service agent in the Customer Sensor organization is an emotional intelligence specialist, supported by AI tools that surface context, suggest responses, flag emotional signals, and manage the operational dimensions of resolution so the agent can focus their energy and expertise on the human dimensions of the interaction.

The most advanced customer service organizations in the Customer Sensor era are designing what might be called "emotional service architectures" — explicit frameworks that define how the service function should respond to each combination of customer lifecycle stage, interaction context, and detected emotional state. These architectures are analogous to medical triage protocols: they provide systematic guidance for allocating the most intensive human attention to the interactions where it will make the greatest difference, while allowing AI to handle interactions where consistency and efficiency are more important than deep emotional engagement.

Department	Primary CxC Matrix Stages	Key Customer Sensor Metrics	Primary AI Application
Executive Management	All stages — strategic oversight	Trust Index, Autonomous Value Index, Customer Sensor Coverage %	AI governance; values alignment monitoring; strategic simulation
Sales	Stages 4-6	Deal velocity,	Predictive

Department	Primary CxC Matrix Stages	Key Customer Sensor Metrics	Primary AI Application
	(Selection through Contract)	configuration accuracy, AI-assisted win rate	opportunity scoring; dynamic configuration; negotiation support
Marketing	Stages 1-3, 15 (Awareness through ID, Community)	Attention quality score, Stage 1-3 conversion, advocacy velocity	Predictive content distribution; behavioral personalization; community intelligence
Customer Service	Stages 11-13 (Use, Care, Repair)	Emotional residue score, first-contact resolution, anticipation rate	Predictive care dispatch; emotional calibration; proactive issue resolution
Product	Stage 11 primarily (Use)	Feature activation rate, autonomous value delivery, adoption depth	Usage intelligence; feature recommendation ; value visibility systems
Finance	Stages 6, 10 (Contract, Payment)	Contact-level P&L, payment option utilization, lifetime value accuracy	Dynamic pricing; contact-level attribution; churn value modeling
Operations	Stages 7-9 (Logistics through Acceptance)	Delivery precision, acceptance quality, benefit-start timing	Logistics optimization; dynamic service tier assignment; acceptance design
HR	Internal — all customer-	CX skill development	Role simulation; performance

Department	Primary CxC Matrix Stages	Key Customer Sensor Metrics	Primary AI Application
	facing roles	index, emotional intelligence scores, quantum empathy training completion	coaching; CX culture assessment
Legal	All stages — regulatory and contractual	Privacy compliance rate, algorithmic ethics audit scores, consent architecture quality	Regulatory monitoring; contract automation; compliance modeling
IT	All stages — infrastructure	Sensor infrastructure uptime, data integration latency, model accuracy	Real-time data integration; AI model management; security monitoring
CRM	All stages — data architecture	Permission depth index, data quality score, prediction accuracy	Unified customer profile; predictive scripting; real-time orchestration

Building Customer Worthy Culture: The Organizational Operating System

The Customer Sensor technology stack, the CxC Matrix 3.0 framework, and the VMAO operating process are necessary but not sufficient for becoming a genuinely Customer Worthy organization. The technical and analytical infrastructure enables the capability. The culture determines whether the capability is exercised in genuine service of customers or in narrow optimization of metrics that approximate but do not fully represent customer value.

The Five Cultural Commitments of Customer Worthy Organizations

Customer Worthy organizations share five cultural commitments that distinguish them from organizations that deploy the same technologies but achieve significantly lower customer value and commercial outcomes:

Cultural Commitment 1: Customers First, Metrics Second

In Customer Worthy organizations, metrics are tools for understanding how well customers are being served — not targets to be optimized independently of customer outcomes. The conversion rate is useful because it reflects whether customers are finding what they need. The cost per interaction is useful because it reflects the efficiency of service delivery. But the moment any metric becomes a target that is optimized independently of the customer outcome it is supposed to represent, it loses its value and potentially becomes harmful.

The cultural commitment to customers first, metrics second is expressed in how organizations respond to situations where metric performance and customer outcome are in conflict. A service team that completes calls quickly to maintain a short average handle time metric at the cost of complete issue resolution has chosen metrics over customers. A marketing team that generates high click-through rates through misleading subject lines that disappoint customers when they open the email has chosen metrics over customers. Customer Worthy organizations have leaders who notice and respond to these conflicts — who recognize that the metric is serving its purpose only when the customer is genuinely well-served.

Cultural Commitment 2: Long-Term Relationships Over Short-Term Transactions

The Customer Sensor infrastructure creates powerful capabilities for short-term revenue optimization — identifying the moments of maximum purchase probability and deploying conversion-optimized interventions at exactly those moments. This capability is commercially valuable when used in service of genuine customer needs. It is commercially counterproductive when used to accelerate transactions that customers would not have initiated on their own timing, because those transactions generate short-term revenue at the cost of the trust and satisfaction that drive long-term lifetime value. This is revenue and growth strategy executed in each interaction with comprehensive value impact analysis and decisioning.

The cultural commitment to long-term relationships over short-term transactions is expressed in how organizations design their optimization targets. Customer Worthy organizations optimize for lifetime value rather than transaction value where business financial modeling justifies, for retention rather than acquisition, and for trust equity rather than conversion rate in any single session. These objectives require accepting lower short-term metrics in some situations — letting a customer leave without purchasing because the moment is not right, investing in a service interaction that exceeds its economic cost ceiling because the relationship value warrants it — in confidence that the long-term economics are superior to the short-term alternative.

Cultural Commitment 3: Genuine Empathy Over Simulated Empathy

The Customer Sensor Mesh infrastructure enables sophisticated simulations of empathy — AI systems that detect emotional states and generate responses calibrated to those states, creating interactions that feel personally attentive even when they are entirely automated. This capability is valuable when it enables organizations to serve more customers better than human empathy alone could achieve at scale. It is problematic when it substitutes for genuine organizational commitment to customer welfare — when the empathy simulation is a surface layer over systems that are fundamentally designed for extraction rather than service.

Genuine empathy means that when the CX system detects that a customer is in distress, the organization's response is genuinely concerned with the customer's welfare — not just with completing a transaction or managing a metric. It means that the emotional calibration in the interaction design reflects authentic care for the customer's experience, not a conversion rate optimization calculation that happens to select for warm tones. Customers are increasingly sophisticated at distinguishing between genuine and simulated empathy, and the brand that is caught simulating empathy it does not actually possess faces reputational consequences that no amount of technical sophistication can repair.

Cultural Commitment 4: Transparency Over Opacity

The Customer Sensor organization knows things about its customers that those customers may not know about themselves — behavioral patterns they haven't noticed, preference structures they haven't articulated, lifecycle trajectories they haven't consciously anticipated. This knowledge is a responsibility as much as an asset. The transparency commitment means sharing relevant knowledge with customers in ways that help them rather than simply using it to optimize extractions from them.

Transparency about AI decision-making, about data collection practices, about the basis for recommendations and offers, creates the informed consent that makes the customer relationship genuine rather than exploitative. Customers who understand why they are receiving specific recommendations can evaluate those recommendations more effectively, trust them more reliably when the recommendation logic is sound, and reject them more confidently when the recommendation does not serve their interests. Transparency makes customers better-equipped participants in their relationship with the organization.

Cultural Commitment 5: Continuous Improvement Over Declared Victory

The most dangerous moment in any CX transformation is the moment when leadership declares success. Success declarations create organizational pressure to defend the current state rather than continue improving it, to suppress negative performance signals that contradict the success narrative, and to reduce investment in the continuous learning and adaptation that keep Customer Sensor systems current and competitive.

Customer Worthy organizations treat every performance improvement as evidence that further improvement is possible, not as a plateau to be maintained. Every customer complaint is an opportunity to improve the system, not a variance to be minimized. Every competitive challenge is an invitation to accelerate capability development, not a threat to be neutralized through lobbying or lock-in strategies. The cultural commitment to continuous improvement is ultimately a commitment to humility — to accepting that the organization never knows enough about its customers, and that the gap between current performance and the best possible performance is always worth closing.

The Customer Sensor Leadership Self-Assessment

Every leader responsible for customer experience in the Customer Sensor era should periodically assess their own leadership against the framework described in this book. The following self-assessment provides a structured reflection tool for that purpose:

Assessment Question	Strong Alignment	Partial Alignment	Needs Development
Do I optimize for customer outcomes or for the metrics that approximate them?	I consistently prioritize genuine customer value over metric performance	I sometimes trade customer value for metric performance	My primary focus is metric performance
Do my teams have genuine cross-functional accountability for matrix cell performance?	Cross-functional teams with shared accountability are active and effective	Some cross-functional collaboration exists but accountability is still primarily departmental	Accountability is primarily departmental; matrix thinking is limited
Is our permission	Customers have granular,	Customers have theoretical	Customer data control is

Assessment Question	Strong Alignment	Partial Alignment	Needs Development
architecture genuinely customer-controlled?	easy-to-use control over all data relationships	control but practical exercise is difficult	primarily compliance-minimum
Do we use AI to serve customers or to extract from them?	All AI applications are evaluated against customer value delivery before deployment	Most AI applications serve customers; some are more extractive	AI optimization primarily serves business metrics without explicit customer value evaluation
Is my organization genuinely improving continuously or defending the status quo?	Continuous improvement is a cultural norm with active organizational support	Improvement is valued but organizational inertia is significant	The primary organizational orientation is defending and maintaining current performance levels

Conclusion

The Customer Worthy Quantum Future — and What's Next

The hand that began this book — with its 100,000 nerves, its 3,000 receptors per fingertip, its ability to synthesize millions of simultaneous signals into a single coherent experience — is not a metaphor for technology. It is a metaphor for intention.

The human hand's extraordinary sensing capability exists not to generate data. It exists to make contact with the world: to build things, to comfort people, to explore, to create, to connect. The sensors are in service of a purpose that transcends sensing. They are how a human being reaches out to another human being and says: I am here, I see you, I can help.

The Customer Sensor economy, at its best, is animated by the same purpose. The sensors, the AI, the digital twins, the autonomous agents — they are not ends in themselves. They are means of reaching customers more completely, understanding them more deeply, serving them more genuinely, and building with them relationships of mutual value that could not exist without the sensing infrastructure to sustain them.

> ***"The Customer Sensor organization of the future is not one that has the most data, or the most sophisticated AI, or the most comprehensive sensor***

> ***network. It is one that uses all of those capabilities in service of the oldest and most enduring purpose of business: to deliver value to the people it serves."***

The CxC Matrix 3.0 is the operational framework for this purpose. Its 90 cells, its 4 cognitive processing layers, its VMAO cycle, its 9 treatment objectives — these are the tools through which organizations translate purpose into practice. They are the architecture of Customer Worthy.

The transformation journey described in this book is not easy. It requires sustained investment, patient learning, genuine organizational change, and the courage to prioritize long-term relationship value over short-term extraction. It requires building trust before it is strictly necessary, because by the time trust is strictly necessary, it is too late to build it. It requires treating customers not as targets but as partners — recognizing that in the Customer Sensor economy, the customer's sensor data, their permission grants, and their AI agents are as much strategic assets as any proprietary technology the organization can develop.

Neil's Tuesday morning — the 17 systems that worked before he woke up, the $212 of value delivered before his first cup of coffee, the frictionless day that resulted from a network of intelligent systems operating in genuine service of his interests — is the destination. The CxC Matrix 3.0 is the map. The work of transformation is the journey.

Begin today. The quantum customer is already waiting.

The Five Commitments of the Customer Worthy Organization

Throughout the preceding chapters, we have built a comprehensive framework for Customer Sensor management — from the foundational principles of the CxC Matrix 3.0 through the practical implementation of wearable experiences, digitally aware environments, and self-programming systems. As we bring this journey to a close, it is useful to distill the framework into its most essential commitments: the five things that the Customer Worthy organization in the sensor era commits to, above and beyond any specific technology deployment or strategic initiative.

Commitment 1: We Will Always Serve the Customer's Actual Interest, Not the System's Optimization Target

The most important commitment in the Customer Sensor era is the one that is hardest to keep: ensuring that the systems you build to serve customers actually do serve customers — that the optimization targets driving AI behavior genuinely align with customer welfare rather than producing customer welfare as a side effect of optimizing for metrics that correlate with it under normal conditions but diverge from it under edge conditions.

This commitment requires constant vigilance. Every optimization system has failure modes. Every metric can be gamed. Every AI system will find the path of least resistance to its objective — and that path may not always be the one the designer intended. The Customer Worthy organization commits to continuous monitoring of system behavior from the customer's perspective, and to prioritizing customer welfare even when the optimization metrics say otherwise.

Commitment 2: We Will Be Transparent About What We Know and What We Do With It

The Customer Sensor organization knows more about its customers than any organization in human history has known about its customers. This knowledge is a responsibility as well as a commercial asset. The Customer Worthy commitment is to exercise that responsibility with genuine transparency: giving customers clear, honest, accessible information about what data is collected, how it is used, and what decisions it influences.

This is not a compliance commitment — it is a values commitment. Transparency that satisfies regulatory requirements while obscuring the reality of data use from customers who cannot parse regulatory language is not genuine transparency. Genuine transparency means that a customer who spends five minutes understanding their data relationship with the organization comes away with an accurate picture of what that relationship entails and how it affects their experience.

Commitment 3: We Will Design for the Long Arc of the Relationship, Not the Next Transaction

The Customer Sensor infrastructure creates unprecedented capability for short-term value extraction: systems that identify vulnerability moments and exploit them, that create artificial urgency to accelerate purchase decisions, that present information in ways that systematically advantage the company at the expense of the customer's informed decision-making. These capabilities are technically available. They are commercially tempting. And they are the precise opposite of Customer Worthy.

The commitment to designing for the long arc means choosing, systematically and consistently, the interaction design that maximizes the lifetime value of the customer relationship — which requires maximizing the customer's genuine satisfaction, informed choice, and confidence that the organization is acting in their interest. Long-arc thinking is not charitable impulse — it is commercial strategy. The customer who trusts you with their wearable data has dramatically higher lifetime value than the customer who purchases once and never grants data permissions. The relationship economy rewards long-arc thinking materially.

Commitment 4: We Will Give Our Customers Meaningful Control

The Customer Sensor organization holds significant power over the customer's experience: it controls what information is surfaced, when, in what context, and to what ends. Meaningful control means sharing that power with the customer — not just providing the theoretical ability to change data settings buried in a settings menu, but genuinely empowering customers to shape their experience, exercise their preferences, and exit relationships that no longer serve them without friction or punishment.

Meaningful control is a competitive advantage in the attention economy. Customers who feel genuinely empowered in their relationship with an organization engage more deeply, share more data, and maintain higher trust levels than customers who feel that their preferences are nominally accommodated while their actual experience is determined by opaque systems. The organization that makes its customers feel genuinely in control has built a loyalty architecture that no competitor can easily replicate.

Commitment 5: We Will Continuously Learn What Customer Worthy Means and Adapt Accordingly

Customer Worthy is not a destination — it is a continuous practice. What it means to genuinely serve customers' interests evolves as technology evolves, as market conditions change, as customers' own capabilities and expectations develop, and as the organization's understanding of what creates genuine value deepens. The final commitment of the Customer Worthy organization is to the process of continuous learning and adaptation — to never declaring victory and to always remaining open to the evidence that current practices can be improved.

This book provides a framework for that practice. The CxC Matrix 3.0 provides the structure. The VMAO cycle provides the operating process. The permission architecture principles provide the ethical guardrails. The Customer Sensor Mesh technologies provide the capabilities. But the framework is only as good as the organizational will to use it in genuine service of the people who trust you with their business, their data, and their time.

> ***"In 2031 and in 2050 and in every year between, the customers who stay, the customers who advocate, and the customers who build communities around your brand***

> ***are the customers who believe that you see them, understand them, and are genuinely working to serve them. Everything else is tactics. That is the strategy."***

The hand with its 100,000 nerves reaches out not to grasp, but to connect. May your Customer Sensor systems do the same.

Appendix A

The CxC Matrix 2.0 Templates and Worksheets

Template 1: Customer Sensor Readiness Assessment

Use this template to assess your organization's current state against the five dimensions of Customer Sensor readiness. Score each dimension on a scale of 1 (no capability) to 5 (fully deployed and optimized).

Dimension	Assessment Questions	Current Score (1-5)	Target Score	Gap Actions
Sensor Infrastructure	Do you have active sensor data from digital, physical, and wearable sources? Are signals integrated into a unified customer data platform?		4-5 by 2027	
AI Analytical Capability	Can you translate sensor signals into real-time customer state models? Do you have causal AI vs. correlational analytics?		4 by 2027	

Dimension	Assessment Questions	Current Score (1-5)	Target Score	Gap Actions
Automation Level	What level (0-5) of CX automation have you achieved? Do you have event-driven pipeline architecture?		Level 3 by 2028	
Permission Architecture	Do customers have granular, legible control over their data? What % of customers have Tier 3+ permission relationships?		>50% Tier 3 by 2027	
Trust Infrastructure	Are your AI systems auditable? Do customers have override capability? Are you compliant with all relevant privacy frameworks?		Full compliance + proactive transparency	

Template 2: CxC Matrix Cell Analysis Worksheet

For each high-priority cell in your CxC Matrix (Stage × Channel), complete this analysis to identify optimization opportunities.

Element	Current State	Target State	Sensor Integration Available	Priority
Perception Layer	What signals are currently captured?	What signals should be captured?	Yes / No / Partial	
Cognition Layer	How are signals currently interpreted?	What AI capability is needed?	Yes / No / Partial	
Actuation Layer	What interventions are triggered?	What responses should be triggered?	Yes / No / Partial	
Emotion Layer	How is emotional state addressed?	What affective computing is needed?	Yes / No / Partial	
Primary Objective	Which of the 9 objectives does this cell currently serve?	Which objectives should it serve?		
Economic Value	What is the current $/interaction for this cell?	What is the target $/interaction?		

Appendix B

AI Prompt Library for Customer Experience Engineers

The following prompts are designed for use with large language model AI systems to support Customer Sensor analysis, strategy development, and experience design. Each prompt is structured to produce actionable output that can be integrated directly into CxC Matrix planning processes.

Strategic Analysis Prompts

Customer Sensor Competitive Assessment

Analyze our competitive landscape in [industry] from a Customer Sensor capability perspective. For each major competitor, identify: (1) known sensor data sources they are utilizing, (2) evidence of AI-driven personalization or automation in their customer experience, (3) permission architecture approach — how do they obtain and manage customer consent?, (4) any public incidents related to privacy or AI ethics that reveal values or capability gaps. Prioritize competitors by their Customer Sensor maturity and identify the two capability gaps most likely to create competitive vulnerability for us in the next 24 months.

CxC Matrix Optimization Analysis

We have provided our current CxC Matrix performance data across [X] lifecycle stages and [Y] channels. For each cell in the matrix: (1) Calculate the current economic value per interaction using the aaCLV formula. (2) Identify which of the 9 treatment objectives are being delivered and which are absent. (3) Score the current Perception, Cognition,

Actuation, and Emotion layer capability on a 1-5 scale. (4) Recommend the three highest-ROI improvements available given our current technology infrastructure. Present results sorted by opportunity value, with implementation complexity as a secondary sort.

Customer Experience Design Prompts

Quantum Empathy Scenario Design

Design a customer experience scenario for the following situation: Customer profile: [describe customer segment and history]. Current lifecycle stage: [stage]. Current emotional state signals: [describe available biometric/behavioral signals]. Simultaneous needs: [list conflicting or complementary needs]. Design an experience response that: (1) honors the full superposition of the customer's emotional state without collapsing it to a single simplified descriptor, (2) advances the customer toward their most important goal, (3) generates measurable business value, and (4) strengthens the long-term relationship. For each element of the design, explain which cognitive processing layer it operates in and which of the 9 treatment objectives it serves.

Privacy-by-Design Data Architecture

We want to deploy Customer Sensor capabilities for [specific use case]. Design a privacy-preserving data architecture that: (1) identifies the minimum necessary data set for the intended customer benefit, (2) specifies which privacy-preserving technologies (ZKP, federated learning, differential privacy, etc.) are appropriate for each data element, (3) designs the customer consent and control framework including granularity of consent, revocation mechanisms, and data access rights, (4) assesses compliance with GDPR, CCPA, and [relevant additional frameworks], and (5) identifies the customer value proposition that justifies data collection — what specific, tangible benefit does the customer receive in exchange for each data element?

Additional Prompt Templates: Advanced Applications

Sector-Specific Prompt Templates

Financial Services: Life Event Prediction and Proactive Outreach

A customer [profile: age, relationship tenure, account types, life stage indicators] has shown the following behavioral signals in the last 90 days: [list behavioral signals from account usage, app interaction, and consent-based data sources]. Please: (1) Identify the three most probable major financial lifecycle events this customer may be approaching in the next 6–18 months, with probability estimates and the specific signals driving each estimate. (2) For each predicted event, design a proactive outreach sequence that: leads with genuine customer value (information or assistance they actually need), positions our relevant products or services in context of that value rather than as the primary message, and is timed to the customer's predicted optimal receptivity window. (3) Define the permission requirements for each element of the proposed outreach and assess our current permission level against each requirement. (4) Estimate the lifetime value impact of successful proactive engagement at each predicted event versus reactive engagement after the event has occurred.

Healthcare: Continuous Care Protocol Design

We are designing a continuous care Customer Sensor program for patients with [condition]. Our wearable monitoring capabilities include: [list sensors and data types]. Our clinical team's time constraints allow for [X] proactive outreach contacts per patient per month. Please: (1) Design a behavioral signal taxonomy that classifies sensor readings into clinical urgency tiers: urgent (requires same-day clinical response), concerning (requires response within 48 hours), monitoring (pattern warrants increased surveillance), and baseline (normal range, no action required). (2) For each urgency tier, design the automated response protocol including patient notification, care team alert, and documentation requirements. (3) Identify the three leading indicators that best predict a transition from monitoring to concerning tier, with the lead time advantage those indicators provide over symptomatic presentation. (4) Design the permission architecture and patient consent framework for this program, including the specific patient benefit proposition for each data type collected. (5) Estimate the clinical outcome improvements and cost reductions based on comparable programs in the literature.

SaaS: Engagement Depth Optimization

Our SaaS product has [X] features organized in [Y] capability tiers. Our customer behavioral data shows: [summarize adoption patterns by customer segment]. Our churn analysis indicates that customers using fewer than [N] features in the first 90 days have [X]% higher churn probability. Please: (1) Design a predictive model specification for identifying customers at 30, 60, and 90 days who are on a low-engagement trajectory. (2) For customers at each trajectory point, design an intervention sequence that: delivers genuine educational value about features relevant to the customer's specific use case, uses behavioral data to time feature introductions to moments of workflow relevance rather than arbitrary calendar timing, and escalates to human success management when automated interventions have not shifted the engagement trajectory after [X] weeks. (3) Design the A/B testing framework for validating the intervention sequence, including success metrics, required sample sizes, and evaluation timeline. (4) Estimate the churn reduction and lifetime value improvement from achieving full intervention sequence deployment.

Implementation Planning Prompts

Transformation Roadmap Development

We are [company description] in the [industry] sector. Our current Customer Sensor maturity level is: Sensor Infrastructure [score/5], AI Analytical Capability [score/5], Automation Level [0-5 scale], Permission Architecture [score/5], Trust Infrastructure [score/5]. Our strategic priorities for the next 3 years are: [list priorities]. Our technology infrastructure includes: [summarize key systems]. Our organizational constraints include: [describe budget, talent, and change management limitations]. Please develop a 36-month Customer Sensor transformation roadmap that: (1) Sequences capability development in the order that maximizes early value delivery while building toward the full target architecture. (2) Identifies the three organizational changes — structural, cultural, or process — that are most critical for roadmap success and recommends timing and approach for each. (3) Estimates the investment required at each phase and the business value delivered by each phase. (4) Identifies the three highest-risk assumptions in the roadmap and designs mitigation approaches for each. (5) Defines the go/no-go criteria for each phase transition.

Customer Sensor ROI Business Case

I need to build a business case for [Customer Sensor capability investment] for [company]. The investment requires [estimated cost]. The proposed capability will affect the following matrix cells: [list cells]. Please build a comprehensive ROI analysis that: (1) Estimates the current economic value (revenue + lifetime value contribution - cost) of each affected matrix cell. (2) Estimates the post-investment economic value of each cell, with the key assumptions underlying each estimate. (3) Calculates the total ROI at 12, 24, and 36 months including implementation costs, ramp-up timing, and maintenance costs. (4) Identifies the three scenarios — optimistic, base, and pessimistic — with the key variable differences that drive each scenario and the probability estimate for each. (5) Identifies the breakeven point and the confidence interval around that estimate. (6) Compares this investment against the opportunity cost of alternative investments of similar scale. Present results in executive summary format suitable for a board-level presentation.

Appendix C

Measurement Frameworks and KPIs

Effective Customer Sensor management requires measurement frameworks that operate at multiple levels of granularity — from individual interaction performance to portfolio-level customer value to organizational transformation progress. This appendix provides the key performance indicators, measurement methodologies, and reporting cadences appropriate for each level.

Level 1: Interaction Performance Metrics

Metric	Definition	Measurement Method	Optimal Reporting Cadence
Attention Quality Score	Composite score of attention duration, engagement depth, and signal richness	Behavioral analytics + biometric weighting where available	Real-time dashboard
Intervention Precision Rate	% of automated interventions that produce the intended customer outcome	A/B testing framework; outcome attribution model	Daily for active experiments; weekly for stable deployments
Anticipation Accuracy	% of proactive service events that customers found genuinely valuable (vs. intrusive or irrelevant)	Post-interaction survey + behavioral confirmation signals	Weekly rolling average

Metric	Definition	Measurement Method	Optimal Reporting Cadence
Permission Depth Index	Weighted average permission tier across the active customer base	CRM permission registry; tier classification algorithm	Monthly
Emotional Residue Score	Net emotional state improvement after interaction vs. before	Pre/post biometric or behavioral signals	Per interaction; aggregate weekly

Level 2: Customer Relationship Metrics

Metric	Definition	Formula
Attention-Adjusted CLV (aaCLV)	Customer lifetime value weighted by attention quality	aaCLV = (AQ × AD × CP × ATV × PF) / CAA
Customer Sensor Depth Score	Completeness of customer sensor coverage across lifecycle stages	(Instrumented stages × Active signals per stage) / (Total stages × Max signals)
Trust Equity Index	Composite measure of customer trust across transparency, control, and perceived fairness	Weighted average of trust dimension scores from periodic assessment
Predictive Value Ratio	Revenue from anticipatory service vs. total CX investment	Anticipatory revenue / Total CX technology + operations cost

The Customer Sensor Measurement Framework: Complete Reference

Effective Customer Sensor management requires a coherent measurement framework that operates across three levels of abstraction: interaction-level metrics that assess the quality of individual touchpoints, relationship-level metrics that assess the health and trajectory of individual customer relationships, and portfolio-level metrics that assess the overall performance of the organization's Customer Sensor investment against strategic objectives.

Interaction-Level Measurement: The Five Dimensions

Every customer interaction in the Customer Sensor framework is evaluated against five dimensions that together provide a complete picture of interaction quality. These five dimensions correspond to the five elements of the CxC Matrix treatment protocol: the customer's state identification, the treatment selection, the delivery quality, the emotional calibration, and the outcome.

Dimension	What It Measures	Primary Metric	Measure-ment Method	Target Standard
State Identification Accuracy	How accurately did the system identify the customer's current state across	Identificati on Accuracy Rate	Comparison of predicted vs. observed customer state indicators	>85% accuracy within ±1 standard deviation

Dimension	What It Measures	Primary Metric	Measure-ment Method	Target Standard
	the four dimensions (identity, state, intent, context)?			
Treatment Precision	How well-matched was the treatment protocol to the customer's identified state and needs?	Treat-ment Rele-vance Score	Post-interaction customer feedback + behavioral outcome correlation	>70% customer confirmation of relevance
Delivery Quality	How effectively was the treatment delivered through the selected channel?	Channel Delivery Score	Technical perform-ance metrics + interaction completion rate	>95% technical completion; >80% engagement rate
Emotional Calibration	How well-matched was the emotional register of the interaction to the customer's emotional state?	Emotional Residue Score	Pre/post emotional signal comparison ; explicit feedback where available	Net positive residue in >75% of interactions
Outcome Achievement	Did the interaction achieve its intended	Objective Achievem ent Rate	Behavioral outcome tracking mapped to	>60% primary objective achievement

Dimension	What It Measures	Primary Metric	Measurement Method	Target Standard
	treatment objectives?		the 9 treatment objectives	per interaction

Relationship-Level Measurement: Lifetime Value Architecture

Relationship-level measurement tracks the health and trajectory of individual customer relationships over time, providing the early warning signals and opportunity identification that enable proactive CX management. The core relationship-level metrics include:

Customer Health Score

The Customer Health Score is a composite metric that integrates multiple behavioral signals into a single number representing the overall health of the customer relationship. It incorporates engagement breadth (how many product features or service dimensions the customer is actively using), engagement depth (how intensively the customer uses the features they have adopted), satisfaction signals (emotional residue scores, explicit feedback, NPS where available), value realization indicators (whether the customer is achieving the outcomes they purchased the product to achieve), and churn risk signals (behavioral patterns correlated with pre-churn behavior in historical data).

The Customer Health Score is most valuable not as an absolute number but as a trajectory indicator — the direction and rate of change in the score over time is more predictive of future behavior than the score at any single point. A customer whose health score has been declining for three consecutive months requires different treatment than a customer whose score has been stable at the same level for a year.

Permission Depth Index

The Permission Depth Index measures the richness and depth of the customer's data relationship with the organization — the extent to which the customer has granted the permission levels that enable the most personalized and anticipatory Customer Sensor experiences. The index is calculated as a weighted average of permission tier levels across all data types in the permission architecture, weighted by the relative predictive value of each data type for the organization's CX capabilities.

The Permission Depth Index is a leading indicator of Customer Sensor capability utilization: customers with higher permission depth levels enable the organization to deliver better personalized experiences, which drives higher satisfaction and loyalty. The relationship is self-reinforcing: better experiences increase trust, trust increases permission depth, higher permission depth enables better experiences. Organizations that actively manage the Permission Depth Index — designing value propositions for each permission tier that make the incremental sharing clearly worthwhile for the customer — build the data richness that enables competitive Customer Sensor performance.

Portfolio-Level Measurement: Strategic Performance

Portfolio-level measurement assesses the overall performance of the Customer Sensor investment against the organization's strategic objectives. The key portfolio-level metrics include:

Portfolio Metric	Definition	Calculation	Strategic Relevance
Customer Sensor ROI	The total economic return from Customer Sensor investment across the full customer portfolio	(Revenue lift + Lifetime value improvement + Cost reduction) / Total CS investment	Primary justification metric for continued CS investment
Competitive Sensing Index	Assessment of CS capability maturity relative to key competitors	Composite score across five CS readiness dimensions relative to competitive benchmark	Strategic planning input; identifies relative capability gaps
Trust Equity Score	The aggregate level of customer trust in the organization's data practices	Weighted composite of transparency, control, accountability, and value exchange scores across customer base	Leading indicator of long-term permission architecture sustainability
Innovation Velocity	The rate at which the organization is developing and deploying new CS capabilities	Number of new CS capabilities deployed per quarter / Average deployment time	Organizational capability health indicator; competitive positioning signal

Portfolio Metric	Definition	Calculation	Strategic Relevance
		from concept to production	
Autonomous Value Ratio	The proportion of total customer value delivered through autonomous CS systems vs. human-initiated processes	Value delivered through automated CS interventions / Total customer value delivered	Operational efficiency metric; automation maturity indicator

The portfolio-level metrics should be reviewed by senior leadership on a quarterly basis, with trend analysis that tracks progress against the transformation roadmap. Organizations that achieve consistent improvement across all five portfolio metrics over a 24–36 month period are building the durable Customer Sensor capabilities that will define competitive advantage in the 2031 and beyond landscape.

Appendix D

Glossary of Customer Sensor Terminology

A

aaCLV (Attention-Adjusted Customer Lifetime Value):

A customer valuation model that weights traditional CLV calculations by the quality and quantity of customer attention interactions. Integrates attention economics into standard revenue forecasting.

Actuation Layer:

The third cognitive processing layer of the CxC Matrix 2.0, responsible for delivering personalized interventions across customer devices and channels based on signals interpreted by the Cognition Layer.

Algorithmic Customer:

A customer whose interactions with an organization are primarily or entirely mediated by AI agents acting on the customer's behalf rather than by the customer directly.

B

Behavioral Signal Processing:

The systematic capture and interpretation of customer behavioral data — clicks, dwell time, navigation patterns, micro-expressions, hesitation signals — to infer current customer state and intent.

Biometric Signal Processing:

The capture and analysis of physiological measurements — heart rate, skin conductance, facial expressions, voice tonality — to assess customer emotional and cognitive states in real time.

Built World Intelligence Threshold:

The projected tipping point in approximately 2033 when commercial and residential built environments routinely integrate sufficient sensor density, edge computing, and AI capability to function as active participants in customer experience delivery.

C

CxC Matrix 3.0:

The expanded version of the Customer Experience CxC Matrix, adding four cognitive processing layers (Perception, Cognition, Actuation, Emotion) and Customer Sensor integration capabilities to the original 15-stage × 6-channel framework.

Customer OS (Customer Operating System):

An individual consumer's coordinated platform of AI agents, data management tools, and autonomous negotiation capabilities that manages marketplace relationships with minimal direct human cognitive investment.

Customer Sensor Mesh:

The interconnected network of connected devices, AI agents, and data streams that surrounds modern consumers and enables anticipatory, autonomous service management.

Customer Sensor Schematic:

A continuously updated computational model and predictive trajectory map for each individual customer, integrating real-time sensor signals with historical behavioral patterns to generate a "play-forward movie" of the customer's relationship trajectory.

D

Digital Twin:

In the Customer Sensor context, a continuously updated computational simulation model of a specific customer that mimics their behavioral patterns, preference structures, and decision-making tendencies with sufficient accuracy to support experience design and optimization planning.

Differential Privacy:

A mathematical technique for adding controlled noise to datasets in a way that makes it impossible to identify individual data subjects while preserving the statistical properties needed for aggregate analysis and AI model training.

E

Emotion Layer:

The fourth cognitive processing layer of the CxC Matrix 2.0, responsible for assessing the customer's emotional state and calibrating the emotional register of interventions accordingly using affective computing and sentiment analysis systems.

Event-Driven Pipeline:

A customer experience architecture in which interactions are triggered automatically by customer events (behavioral signals, lifecycle transitions, sensor readings) according to pre-defined rules, rather than by scheduled campaigns or human initiation.

F

Federated Learning:

A machine learning approach in which AI models are trained on data that resides on customers' devices rather than being centralized in company infrastructure. The model learns from the data without the data leaving the device.

Femtosecond Economy:

The emerging market paradigm in which customer attention is measured, valued, and optimized at sub-second resolution, with economic value assigned to individual millisecond-level interaction events.

H

Homomorphic Encryption:

An encryption technique that allows mathematical operations to be performed on encrypted data without first decrypting it, enabling organizations to process sensitive customer data without ever having access to the unencrypted information.

M

MCP (Model Context Protocol):

The emerging standard for machine-to-machine communication that allows AI systems to discover, negotiate with, and transact through other AI systems, enabling autonomous agent-to-agent commerce.

Mission-Infused Micro-Engagement:

A customer interaction designed at the micro or nano-slot level to simultaneously serve the customer's immediate need and advance a specific business objective, in service of the organization's broader mission.

P

Permission Architecture:

The layered consent framework governing what autonomous actions AI agents may take on a customer's behalf, defining four tiers of autonomy from Tier 1 (monitor and report only) to Tier 4 (broad autonomous authority with human override available).

Perception Layer:

The first cognitive processing layer of the CxC Matrix 2.0, responsible for capturing raw signals from all customer channels and devices and translating them into structured data for analysis.

Q

Quantum Empathy:

The capacity to hold multiple, potentially contradictory understandings of a customer's emotional and motivational state simultaneously, and to respond in ways that honor that complexity rather than collapsing it to a single simplified descriptor.

Quantum Slot:

In the CxC Matrix 2.0 slot taxonomy, a predictive opportunity that exists before customer conscious awareness — the window of optimal receptivity predicted by behavioral models based on time, activity patterns, and historical response data.

V

VMAO Cycle (Visualize, Monetize, Analyze, Optimize):

The four-step continuous improvement process that drives the CxC Matrix operating system. In the Customer Sensor framework, each step is AI-enhanced to operate at machine speed rather than quarterly cadence.

W

Wearable Intelligence Threshold:

The projected tipping point in approximately 2031 when wearable devices routinely carry sufficient processing power, sensor breadth, and AI capability to serve as primary interfaces for Customer Sensor experience delivery, replacing smartphones as the dominant personal computing platform.

Z

Zero-Knowledge Proof (ZKP):

A cryptographic method that allows one party to verify to another party that a statement is true, without conveying any information beyond the truth of the statement. Used in Customer Sensor applications to verify customer eligibility or attributes without revealing the underlying data.

Appendix E

The 2031-2055 Customer Technology Timeline

The following timeline represents the most probable trajectory of Customer Sensor Mesh technology development and market adoption from today through 3038, based on current technology development trajectories, capital investment patterns, and regulatory trends as of today. Events before 2031 represent projections with moderate-to-high confidence. Events after 2038 represent speculative extrapolations intended to stimulate strategic thinking rather than reliable forecasts.

Today-2029: Foundation Phase

- 2028: MCP achieves critical mass as machine-to-machine commerce standard; agent-to-agent transactions represent 12% of B2C commerce volume in leading sectors
- 2028: Privacy-preserving personalization techniques (federated learning, ZKP) move from research to enterprise deployment in healthcare and financial services
- 2029: Built environment sensor integration reaches 30% of new commercial construction in developed markets; ambient retail intelligence mainstream in premium retail
- 2029: AR glasses achieve mass-market price threshold ($299); spatial computing transitions from enterprise to consumer mainstream

- 2028: Customer OS platforms launched by major technology platform companies; first generation of integrated personal AI agent ecosystems

2028-2035: Acceleration Phase

- 2030: Level 3 CX automation mainstream in financial services, telecommunications, and e-commerce; human agents handle exceptions and complex consultative interactions
- 2031: Wearable biometric monitoring achieves medical-grade accuracy for common health parameters; healthcare Customer Sensor applications achieve clinical validation
- 2030: Neural interface peripherals enter consumer market; thought-adjacent interaction available through commercial devices for the first time
- 2032: Built World Intelligence Index launches; commercial real estate marketed on sensor integration scores alongside traditional metrics
- 2031: Agent-to-agent commerce represents >35% of consumer transaction volume in advanced markets; traditional web-based shopping interfaces begin significant decline

2036-2040: Threshold Phase

- 2036: Wearable Intelligence Threshold achieved; wearables become primary CX delivery channel, surpassing smartphones in daily interaction count
- 2037: MCP becomes universal commerce standard; companies without machine-readable product APIs lose access to automated purchasing systems

- 2038: First Level 4 CX systems deployed at scale; virtual elimination of routine human-handled customer interactions in instrumented organizations
- 2036: Built World Intelligence Threshold achieved; ambient environment becomes standard CX delivery surface in commercial and premium residential contexts
- 2037: Predictive wearable intelligence achieves 4-8 hour need anticipation accuracy at commercial deployment scale

2040-2045: Maturation Phase

- 2041: Neural interface mainstream; thought-to-action latency <200ms; cognitive experience design emerges as primary UX discipline
- 2041: Level 4 CX automation near-universal in enterprise customer service; human CX roles concentrate in values governance, complex consultation, and emotional service
- 2040: Quantum computing achieves commercial viability for customer experience simulation; CX systems that model millions of customer futures before choosing interventions
- 2042: Synthetic customer communities — digital twins of customer segments — used routinely for experience design testing without involving real customers
- 2044: Ambient intelligence ubiquity; Level 5 self-programming CX systems in pilot deployment; humans begin transition to AI values custodian role

2045-2055: Speculative Future

The following projections are explicitly speculative, intended to stimulate long-horizon strategic thinking rather than reliable technology forecasting. They represent extrapolations of current trends rather than predictions.

- 2047: Level 5 self-programming CX systems in broad enterprise deployment; organizations hire "AI Alignment Officers" responsible for ensuring CX system objectives remain aligned with human values
- 2048: Physical and digital experience fully integrated; the concept of "channel" becomes obsolete as experience architecture is designed for consciousness rather than devices
- 2050: Quantum-enhanced CX simulation routinely models complete customer lifetime trajectories; intervention design optimizes for multi-decade relationship outcomes
- 2051: Synthetic experience generation mainstream; significant portion of consumer "experiences" are AI-generated simulations indistinguishable from physical reality
- 2054: Customer relationship management has dissolved into general life management; the CxC Matrix has evolved into a universal framework for human-AI value co-creation
- 2055: The horizon of meaningful extrapolation. Whatever "customer experience" means at this point, the principles that have always defined it — genuine understanding of human needs, ethical value exchange, trust-based relationships, continuous learning and improvement — will still be relevant. The tools will be unimaginable. The purpose will be unchanged.

End of Appendices

Customer Worthy: Customer Sensor

www.ingramcontent.com/pod-product-compliance
Lightning Source LLC
LaVergne TN
LVHW052251200926
848481LV00002B/333